Synthetic Reality

合 成 现 实

timezone **8**

"Making Noise in the West, to Attack in the East".

Marianne Brouwer

This is a story from the mid-eighties: a young Chinese artist who had emigrated to Paris went to see Zao Wou Ki, the grand old master of the "Ecole de Paris". Zao Wou Ki was famous for his abstract paintings, which were landscape-like with some reminiscence of Chinese brushpainting. The artist asked Zao Wou Ki what he had to do to make his way in the West. Zao Wou Ki told him: "never speak a word of Chinese anymore, never speak to anyone Chinese. Forget that you are Chinese altogether. Then, perhaps, you will make it in the West". At the time this attitude was common. Who, for example, cared whether surrealist painter Wilfredo Lam was of Cuban origin or attached any importance to the fact that conceptual artist Stanley Brouwn came from Suriname (Dutch Guyana)? Their work was part of modern art, which, though of Western origin, was seen as the only truly international art. To some, this view referred to modern art's critical potential, to its revolutionary origins in Dada, Futurism and Constructivism, to others to Modernism's value-free status as "autonomous art". This state of affairs, which was actually a state of mind, started to change around the mid-seventies. A new generation of artists had arrived, many of whom were refugees - I recall the first wave of exiled artists from South America for instance. Others who had been born elsewhere - often in former colonies - came to study in the West; yet others had been born of immigrant parents. Theirs was a different attitude altogether, calling attention to the non-Western contextuality of their work and its political importance. They were soon to be joined by contemporary artists working in non-Western countries, Chinese artists among them. However, due to the growing influx of immigrants and refugees in most Western countries during the past decades on the one hand, and the aftermath of "nine-eleven" on the other, the rise of a multi- or transculturalism has been countered by the hardening of immigration laws, police regulations and political cant, spurred by a growingly popular xenophobia. They stand in stark contrast to the increasingly successful and prestigious "globalization" of art as seen in an increasing number of international exhibitions all over the world.

To understand the extraordinary success of Chinese contemporary art in the West throughout the past decade, we have to remember the context of the time: the end of the Cultural Revolution in 1976 and the fall of Maoism were short-term history; the fall of the Berlin Wall had announced the "end of Marxism and Communism", and the establishment of a global economy, as well as the rise of China as a future economic super power, came to mark the new era.

The exhibition "Magiciens de la Terre" at the Centre Pompidou in Paris in 1989, symbolically marked the arrival of globalism in contemporary art. The opening of the exhibition almost coincided with the tragedy of Tian An Men Square. For the first time, the art world in the West was confronted with contemporary art from all over the globe, including works by three Chinese artists: Huang Yongping, Yang Jiechang and Gu Dexin. As a consequence China was "in" -had arrived- almost overnight. Just a few years later, launched in 1992, the touring exhibition "China Avant-Garde" met with an overwhelming success in Europe. It was the first overview of Chinese contemporary art ever, exhibiting an expert choice and a tremendous variety of works by some ninety artists living in China or abroad. That expertise came mainly from Hans van Dijk, the Dutch gallerist and art-lover who had lived in

China for over twenty-five years, ceaselessly struggling to support Chinese contemporary art from within China itself.

Suddenly the art world discovered that Chinese art no longer automatically implied calligraphy and brush painting or Socialist Realism, but that a new phenomenon had developed since the death of the Cultural Revolution. Starting with the "Generation of 85" Chinese art had become installation art, conceptual art, political painting, and more: an art which made use of Western art idioms, but had recreated or reinvented them from scratch to suit its own necessities and traditions. This art was unmistakably Chinese, but unlike anything seen before. As it became clear that quite a number of artists and critics responsible had left their native country just before or soon after the happenings of 1989 it was soon understood that this kind of art was unsanctioned in China officially. From those days the development of Chinese contemporary art has been marked by two distinct currents: developments growing up within China, and those being developed outside.

Inside China artists struggled to get their works exhibited, to circumvent censorship and draw the attention of any ambulant curators and collectors to be found, while abroad a Chinese hype was going on in Biennials, Triennials and many other exhibitions. In the West an altogether different struggle was going on contested along two fronts at once. The emigrated artists and art critics worked tirelessly for the recognition of Chinese contemporary art, both in the West and in China. I particularly recall Chen Zhen, Huang Yongping, Cai Guo Qiang, Gu Wenda, Ming, Yang Jieqiang, and the critics Hou Hanru and Fei DaWei. Chen Zhen was fond of using statements from the famous book "The 36 Stratagems" as titles for his works, sometimes changing them around to suit his own policy. Thus he reversed the sixth Stratagem ("Making Noise in the East, to Attack in the West") into "Making Noise in the West, to Attack in the East". He wanted to indicate that through becoming famous in the West, Chinese artists should strive to legitimize contemporary art within China.

Another of Chen Zhen's sayings was: "living in the West as a Chinese artist, is like having two cultures, two libraries, two armies". This referred to the necessity for artists abroad to make their art comprehensible to a Western audience, to "translate" China for the West. Since the eighties the question of "translation" has been a major one in the works of most non-Western artists living in the West. Unfortunately it has not received the theoretical attention it deserves, mainly, I believe, because Western art critics tend not to know what is meant, i.e. the problem being addressed. The West has its own system in which art works circulate and are understood, and it generally believes - understandably but equally incorrectly- that this system is the only possible model. If an artwork is to be interpreted for what the artist wants it to mean s/he is almost obliged to create a context or "translational system" which makes it possible that the work's very existence be "read" and understood in alternate - possibly contrary - cultural terms. Comprehension, however, may not be the real target (I speculate) and errors and faulty readings are part of the reception in the West of much "art from elsewhere" without many people seeming to care, as long as the artist promises to be hot or famous, in short, a trophy still. For example, when Cai Guo Qiang proposed a gun powder performance for my exhibition "Heart of Darkness" in 1994, this included uprooting a number of trees in the grounds surrounding the museum and replanting them upside down. One critic read this to literally mean "uprootedness", in the sense of homelessness, exile. Actually the work demonstrated the Taoist concept of healing a world that is out of joint or in turmoil, by stopping and reversing time. For it seems to be a well-known phenomenon that trees replanted upside-down may take root anew from their crowns and continue growing.

The story of Zao Wou Ki and an anxious student I began with may help illustrate the enormous gap that existed between modern art in the West and the rise of a modern art elsewhere in the world, well into the eighties. Hopefully it can also illuminate the gap that resulted from the image the art world had of what Modern art was or should be - i.e. actively needed to represent - and its incomprehension for the processes of modernity that needed to happen elsewhere over the globe. In other words: in Western eyes modern art WAS the West. One of the consequences of this point of view was the voyeuristic appreciation of "Eastern" dissident art through Western eyes. The notion that freedom of expression was the exclusive, historical achievement of Western society since the Enlightenment, led to the inverse reasoning that all art from repressed countries like Russia or China had to be "dissident" in order to be "authentic".

This point of view was not due to any real understanding of Russian or Chinese contemporary art. Neither was it due, as I will argue, to any real understanding of contemporary art movements in the West, quite the contrary. Western authorities, critics, the art world, have an interest in passing over or smoothing out the deeper meanings of an independent art, comparable to any non-democratic regime. However, the clamour for dissident art led to the bizarre situation that for a while Chinese artists who wanted to make money only had to title their shows "Dissident painting from China" and the Mercedes was ready to be parked in front of the newly refurbished Hutong. It is typical that these shows were supported by the kind of conservative galleries and art collectors, both Western and Chinese, who like to invest their money in painting as such, rather than in cumbersome installations or any other intellectually "difficult" art. Even though "Political Pop" was appreciated as part of the category of "dissident" art, the key to its success in the West was not due to its content but the fact that it was (oil) painting, and therefore represented tradition, historical and thus material value.

What happened to Russian art after 1989 may serve as a sampler of the future, once dissidence is no longer an issue on the (further) Eastern front. After the fall of the Berlin Wall, the prominent auction house Sotheby decided to hold an auction in Moscow of "Perestroika Painting". International buyers flocked to the event, the works were sold at fabulous prices - it is safe to say that the auction was an immense success. It is also probably safe to say that it killed off positive aspects of the uniquely indigenous contemporary art production(s) in Russia for a long time to come. For years, Russian artists had developed codes of meaning within their works to circumvent censorship and to communicate with one another. The international crowd of art shoppers and investors wasn't interested in the CONTENT of the paintings. The Russian artists who had hoped to see their long term struggle understood, their issues to be out in the open and appreciated by the West, saw themselves robbed instead of everything they had wanted to say and believed in. I believe that some of the more aggressive phenomena in Russian art in recent years can be traced back to a feeling of invisibility or powerlessness that settled in during that time.

If dissidence was a prime issue in this (diplomatic) game, Orientalism was - and has been for a long time - a deep-rooted issue. Basically it comes in two different guises. There is the Western expectation that Chinese contemporary art must conform to a continuation, if only in some formal way, of Chinese historical art; otherwise, what's Chinese? On the other hand, many Western critics have expressed disappointment in recent Chinese installation and video art - their disappointment representing the other face of the same coin in fact. Since video art, in particular, uses "Western" technology it is viewed, for that reason alone, as relatively uninteresting, even opportunistic. At times it is implied that this art is specifically intended for export to the West, which, of course, may be true in certain cases, just as it may also be true that some artists play on Western expectations of the exotic. Ignorance of what actually goes on in China, what this or any of the other art forms represent, partly explains the lack of judgment on the part of Western art critics. Another, more principled reason is to be found in Western art theory's concern regarding the autonomy of art. From the pro-autonomy point of view Modernism cannot be synonymous with modernity, because it considers art to be almost transcendentally value-free, independent of any social, political, economic or even cultural context.

Both installation art and video art have become a worldwide "lingua franca" over the past years, a language - rather a grammar - that could be practised throughout the world, each work speaking its own local language or dialect, yet still to be understood by anyone. Ironically, the focus by the Chinese authorities on calligraphy and brush painting as the official State art is consistent with the Western argument for a value-free art: both promoting a neutered formalism as free expression. Colonialist and Orientalist views on Chinese culture become almost interchangeable therein. During the fifties a similar argument of autonomy was made the foundation of the political promotion of American Abstract Expressionism by the United States. A provocative book entitled "How New York Stole the Idea of Modern Art" proved beyond a doubt that Abstract Expressionism was used by the CIA for American propaganda in Europe after World War II, based on the argument of its value-free, transcendental quality. Time and again, arguments of Empire have used art to further its own targets. Time and again, artists have invented strategies of independence to prevent, forestall or counter this state of affairs.

In the early eighties, almost overnight, the word "politics" was no longer allowed in art. We were to concentrate again on painting and sculpture, on oil and bronze, on style and all the other Old Values. This was the time of "Wild Painting" and the "Trans avant-gardes". Performance and video art almost disappeared from the art-scene. Politics had become THE non-word, the taboo for a younger generation that apparently was fed up with the "do-gooders" of the seventies and the sixties, and who wanted to strike it rich for once, not be disenfranchised again when money talked. "Post-Modernism" became the eclectic new term for everything that went on.

1984, however, saw the start of a debate that would have considerable consequences. This was the so-called "Primitivism" debate, following the show "'Primitivism' in Twentieth Century Art, Affinity of the Tribal and the Modern" at MOMA in New York. Curated by William Rubin and Kirk Varnedoe of the New York Museum of Modern Art, this was an art-historical exhibition in which Western art works were exhibited with the non-Western art by which they had been inspired. There were Cubist and Surrealist paintings, works by Giacometti, Max Ernst, Cezanne and so on. These works figured as the stars in the exhibition; they were shown on the first floor of MOMA, well lit, beautifully spaced. The so-called "primitive" works - African, Oceanian, Cycladic, Kwakiutl and many other works from non-Western, mainly black and Pacific cultures-were displayed by the entrance. They were barely annotated, displayed in badly lit vitrines and, in general, looked as if they didn't matter all that much except to serve as art-historical or ethnological cues to the Western masters on the floor above. The show also included a separate section of more recent art works by a younger generation of Western artists, including Eva Hesse, Robert Smithson, and Richard Long; strangely, no affinity with non-Western art could actually be proven. In fact, as the American art critic Thomas McEvilley argued in his brilliant attack on the show, those works were shown with the sole objective of proving that: "'Primitivism' was a current in Modernist art while "'Primitive', in turn designates the actual tribal objects [....]. No attempt is made [in the show] to recover an emic, or inside, sense of what primitive esthetics really were or are". According to McEvilley the "primitive" represents something the curators actually dreaded. Hence the exclusion of such obviously qualified artists as Jospeh Beuys or Paul McCarthy from the separate section. The catalogue essay by curator Kirk Varnedoe states that "the ideal of regression closer to nature is dangerously loaded" and that such works bring up "uncomfortable questions about the ultimate content of all ideals that propose escape from Western tradition into a primitive state". McEvilley counters: "The primitive, in other words, is to be censored out for the sake of Western civilization" to conclude: "'Primitivism'" [the exhibition] lays bare the way our cultural institutions relate to foreign cultures, revealing it as an ethnocentric subjectivity inflated to co-opt such cultures and their objects into itself [....] My real concern is that this exhibition shows Western egotism still as unbridled as in the centuries of colonialism and souvenirism".

MOMA's censorship of the "primitive" in Western art was, like all censorship, based on fear. It won't do to underestimate that fear, because it runs like a long undercurrent through Western civilization. The nature of that fear is the haunting theme of Joseph Conrad's ambiguous novel "Heart of Darkness", which is set in the Belgian Congo at the beginning of the 20th century. The image of the Congo in "Heart of Darkness" is not an image of any real Africa; it is a map of fear, the sombre delirium of an Empire hallucinating what it represses most. A deep fissure runs through "Heart of Darkness", as though a secret awareness of betrayal and self-loathing becomes the infamous and mocking double of the author's patriotism, his adopted Britishness. Not for nothing was its theme adopted by Coppola's film "Apocalypse Now", where it is set in Vietnam. The theme of man's "dark side", of natural man as inherently evil, of natural society as a society of greed, war and violence, has haunted Western civilization since the Enlightenment. It was seen as the consequence of the doctrine of the free will and the loss of religious and worldly moral authority that accompanied the rise of capitalism and liberal democracy. It was first given a voice by Thomas Hobbes, the 18th century English author, in his book "Leviathan". The opposite side of the argument is of course represented by Rousseau's belief in the "noble savage", that is to say in the inherent goodness of natural man. To give an inkling of the sincerity of his revolutionary rhetorics; a recent study shows that Rousseau was very much aware of the slave trade, yet never took the risk of actually demanding its abolition.

What is interesting and very revealing about McEvilley's point of view in the "Primitivism" debate is, that it showed the link between the fear of the "primitive" to the fear of radical, or subversive, Western contemporary art itself. That is to say, to the deeply problematic and critical issues in our own society that art is capable of bringing up and representing. Rather unexpectedly, here was proof that colonialism, and the official, State or national representation of the arts, are linked together by the effort of editing out "The Other".

If art in the West has come to be seen as a manifestation of "Otherness", which in the worst case may be interpreted as the symptom of a sick society (most prominently expressed by the nazi-term "Entartete Kunst" or "Degenerate Art"), art emerging in a Third World context comprises a double threat of "Otherness". The Figure of the "Other" is the single most challenging mythical figure to combat for non-Western artists and intellectuals alike. However, it is also the most important myth to combat in Western art itself, if it is to be taken seriously as a critical art.

For a while it seemed that these two notions could meet in post-Modernist theory and its emerging companions: "Cultural Studies" and studies of "Visual Culture" as the way out of a eurocentric, neo-colonial Modernism, in favour of a theory of "Otherness", which would be capable of including both Western and non-Western contemporary art. Thanks to critics like McEvilley post-Modernism briefly became the meeting point between French philosophy, Foucault, Derrida, Lyotard, Deleuze-Guattari, between theories of deconstruction, nomadism, the rhizome, etcetera, in Western and non-Western contemporary art. However, there also lay its weakness, for post-Modernism by itself was not strong enough a theory. It basically remained a eurocentric, or Western-based theory, too eclectic, too easily satisfied with all sorts of bad or good art, too much focused on the exotic side of "multicultural" art, to be able to deal with the many issues of non-Western contemporary art, and their specific histories and iconographies.

These weaknesses came to bear very heavily on the exhibition "Magiciens de la Terre", already mentioned. The show was curated by Jean Hubert Martin, then director of the Museum of Modern Art in the Centre Pompidou in Paris. It was intended as the definitive reply to the "Primitivism" exhibition, meant to exorcise the fear of "The Other" by bringing together contemporary art from all parts of the world on an equal footing. Curators, artists, gallerists, were sent to the remotest corners of the world to scout for contemporary art in the making. It was a huge, grandiose show, full of works that had never been seen, by artists never heard of before. It immediately opened up an immense gap in the art market. It was also, unfortunately, a very naive show. Suffice it to say, that its main flaw - unforgivable - was that no context was provided for non-Western works, the dominance of Western art was very visible, and that the show collapsed under the very phenomena it had wanted to combat. There was a storm of criticism and Jean-Hubert Martin was fired from his position as director within a year. Nonetheless, we have "Magiciens de la Terre" to thank for the many non-Western artists who have become part of the international art world and for the many different shows that have tried to do better since then. Yet "Magiciens" still must share the blame for the resulting "non-Western art" hype in all sorts of Biennials and Triennials, when famed museum directors or "independent curators" go on flying tours to select one or two "new" artists from Mexico, China, Senegal or what you will, who then become the next hot thing. Artists as always are left to make the best of this situation, and devise ways in which their work can be seen and understood as intended.

Which brings me to a very different history, far more slow and hidden, which runs parallel to this first post-Modernist, multiculturalist phase in contemporary Western art, but has been very different from it. I refer to the history of the long and hard road traveled by non-Western, immigrant and indigenous artists themselves. It was much less fun or willfully eclectic, a struggle that still has to deal with all forms of racism, xenophobia, ignorance and exclusion. This history has depended on the pioneering work of small clusters of courageous artists, theoreticians and collective initiatives, like "Third Text", the transcultural art magazine edited by Rasheed Araeen and Jean Fisher, to name but one very important example.

Fortunately, their efforts have been reinforced by the growing amount of research in other fields: history and sociology, cultural studies, and literary theory. We have witnessed the uncovering of black slavery's history, no longer just to ignore, or the research into the influence of black culture on the Americas. Similarly, the writings of Edward Said on Orientalism and Cultural Imperialism, or the theories of "Otherness" developed by Homi Bhabha and Gayatri Chakravorty Spivak. Artists are publishing their own critical texts; I particularly recall the pioneering writings by Jimmy Durham and Trin Minh Ha. Today there is an enormous amount of literature available, and it is hard to plead ignorance for want of material. What is more encouraging, even, is the growing amount of international and intercultural exchange between artists, young artists especially, and curators, and the growing interest in transcultural studies in art academies. Curators today come from all sorts of countries and cultures, from Pakistan, India, Mexico, Japan, South Africa, etcetera, and they are being asked to curate important and prestigious shows. Theories of globalization and modernity are being developed, that may one day have a decisive influence, not only in art but hopefully in politics as well.

With all this, you would think that the domestic situation in Western countries has significantly improved. But xenophobia has recently spread much wider in Europe, and the general feeling is rapidly being polarized between "them and us". Suffice it to recall the rise of populist and ultra right wing movements. All the worse, therefore, is the silence and indifference of those voices that have the authority to change the perception of the general reader; most "official" art critics and journalists do not think it worth their while to commit themselves to any serious investigation in "art from elsewhere", keeping politics and ideological debate out of art still.

Non-Western artists are participating in art manifestations everywhere; from that point of view there has been progress indeed. But it is a very fragile process, because a lot of it is ad hoc and subjected to rapid amnesia. Much theoretical work has been done, almost all of it by non-Western intellectuals, artists and critics. Most of it has concentrated on the direct necessity of creating an understanding of, fighting for and introducing the art of "The Other". But much more is needed. We need records, research, books and anthologies. We need to decentralize the power centers of the arts. We need informed Western art critics and collectors. We very much need research into and records of the historical developments of modernity, Modernism and contemporary art in countries all over the world. Critical debates are going on in China between various artists and critics. But the history of Chinese modern and contemporary art remains yet to be written from the Chinese point of view. Even Japan, with its long history of Westernization, its modern life-style and contemporary art and architecture, has never produced an anthology of modern Japanese art of its own. Who today can say who the real heirs of the Mexican socialist mural painters are? Who today is aware, that in the fifties and early sixties there was the buddings of a genuine modernity in India, Egypt, Turkey and Iran? Today we should start collecting and writing the many histories of modernity, before they are entirely forgotten or lost. And I mean that these should come from those centers and countries themselves. In order to grasp the many developments in non-Western art we see today, there is a real need to develop the understanding of their origins and their contexts, their many inscriptions and iconographies.

Is the Chinese hype all but over in the West? No shows like "China Avant-Garde" or "Another Long March" have been held for quite a while even though a growing number of Chinese artists are included in the Venice Biennial and in Documenta. But the time is now past in which collective exhibitions of the genre "Twenty painters from Taiwan" or "Three women artists from Ghana" were useful curatorial tools. Today, it is not just quantity that counts. It is all the more important that shows like "Synthetic Reality", specialized exhibitions made with passion, curatorial precision and first-hand historical knowledge, be made both inside and outside China. Through them, the history of Chinese contemporary art will gradually be able to shape itself. There is a long road ahead for Chinese artists and critics alike.

Synthetic Realities

Els van der Plas

A video by Chen Shaoxiong (1962, Guangzhou) shows a lithe skyscraper dodging an accelerating plane. This image evokes both immediate recognition post 9/11 and the surprise of a building that moves. Shaoxiong's work concerns present-day international terrorism and visual manipulation. The title *Windows 2002* refers not only to the windows in New York from where the catastrophe was observed but also to Bill Gates' Windows program. Was what we saw genuine? Or could it have been the result of computer manipulation? Virtual realities are playing an increasingly important role in contemporary society.

Synthetic Reality in Context 1

Topical subjects and images defined the *Synthetic Realities* exhibition of Rectember 2002 where a plethora of video, digital media and sound filled the East Modern Art Centre (EMAC) in Beijing. This large, unfurnished and factory-like space had been transformed into a hip, new media show. Visitors were bombarded with video images and strange sounds, and were overwhelmed by the exhibition. Here, there could be no 'dictatorship of the viewer', to quote the theme of the 2003 Venice Biennale that included Chen Shaoxiong. Instead viewers surrendered themselves to the power of image and space.

Synthetic Realities was one of the first exhibitions in China to be completely devoted to video and the manipulated image. These 'avant-garde' artists, including Chen, are now almost forty and have had a defining influence both on the Chinese art world and beyond. They were the founders and members of the '85 Movement, which is also known as the New Wave, and were the first generation of artists to graduate after the Cultural Revolution and to devote themselves to creative freedom and critical analysis. They were also the initiators of the 1989 *China Avant-Garde* exhibition at the China Art Gallery in Beijing, which the government shut down on its opening day after two artists started shooting at their work. They were not firing blanks either literally or metaphorically, and *China Avant-Garde* was the result of years of making underground and alternative art that deployed various media and disciplines. Performance, video and conceptual art found their way to China at a time when Chinese society was gripped by a sense of hope and expectation. The Cultural Revolution was over, the borders had opened slightly and reality was becoming increasingly real. It was no longer a question of making state art or traditional painting. Instead artists set fire to their work (Xiamen, 1986) or threw the standard work on Chinese art history into a washing machine together with its Western equivalent A Concise History of Modern Painting and then publicly exhibited the crumpled results (Huang Yong Ping, 1987). This energetic cultural explosion reached both its zenith and its turning point at the *China Avant-Garde* show of 1989.

These cultural developments in a nutshell have left their mark on the Chinese art world. This mixture of openness and Western influences, increasing censorship and oppression created a generation of artists with an ambivalent attitude towards reality. What is real or genuine, and for whom is a particular reality intended? After the Cultural Revolution, one of the most important questions for Chinese artists concerned the way in which they related to everyday reality. And what does that everyday reality mean in a country that is characterised by a lack of freedom of opinion? *Synthetic Realities* is both a consequence of this and a preview of what may be in store.

The Big Brother and None-Event

The *Synthetic Realities* exhibition provided the artist Geng Jianyi with the opportunity to explore the boundaries of the reality of an exhibition. The show became the subject of a journalistic investigation into what took place behind the scenes of this exhibition. Who were the artists? How did they live? What is the practice of creating a show like? In *Beyond Synthetic Reality*, Geng Jianyi presented nine journalistic portraits of the nine participants, each of which was shown on a monitor. *Beyond Synthetic Reality* focused on 'the making' and 'the makers' of this exhibition. It was slightly reminiscent of an art version of Big Brother or a Reality TV program on artists. Zhu Jia (1963, Beijing) showed virtually the opposite of the Big Brother principle. *Double Landscape* (2002) is a 16 mm film where a young man sits at a table and drinks his coffee. We see blocks of flats in a city through a window behind him. A lady is standing in front of him. The viewer sees her back. Is she a waitress? Is she his girlfriend? Although the viewer does not realise it, it is in fact a dummy. The man drinking coffee is caught between two fake realities: the plastic shop-window dummy and the modernised city that appears to have no relation to the past but merely expresses the boredom of modernity. Nothing actually happens in this film: the man drinks his coffee, the city exists and the woman is a motionless dummy. Here, Reality TV has degenerated into the ultimate image of tedium.

The None-Event and Surrealist Approach

Li Yongbin (1963, Beijing) has created another 'non-event' that is entitled the *Sun* and consists of a one-hour video loop of a window through which the rays of the winter sun are shining. This lethargic image is accompanied by a piece by Bach that is played at 50% of the normal speed. Li Yongbin seems to be saying that reality is no more exciting than this. He previously showed the beauty of slow living by reflecting his face in a bowl of black ink. The movement of the fluid transforms Narcissus into a monster who is recorded on video in *Face III* (1997). In *Face I* Li mixes a self-portrait with the portrait of an old woman. What are you looking at? Is it an old person or a young person, a man or a woman? These simple video manipulations are typical of Yongbin's work. It is not what you see. It is not a pipe, wrote the surrealist Magritte on his painting of a pipe.

Wang Gongxin's Go Beyond is another surrealist reality. It consists of a video projection and a photo on a light box. The photo is of the artist cycling through a suburb of Beijing. The video shows the naked artist falling through the air and landing in New York to be followed by a pile of clothes and the bike, which is apparently the same one as on the photo. Filmic vocabularies, particularly those of science-fiction films, are used in the various media, such as the photo, the moving images and the sound, and also in the spatial sense of being both here and there. *Go Beyond* dramatises the artist's experiences in Beijing and New York, two of the world's most important cities, and focuses on subjects such as migration and urban life.

Shi Yong has been involved for some time with the depiction of reality as 'image'. He translates a magnified reality, a cliche, in his manipulated, photographic self-portraits as a businessman and in his work *New Image of Shanghai* Today where viewers use the Internet to select the hairstyles and suits of a Chinese man. The question here is: 'What does the new man of Shanghai look like?' Viewers can create their own realities.

At *Synthetic Realities*, Shi Yong exhibited his audio-visual installation *QQ's Illusion*. It consists of a person gesturing wildly on a polythene film screen. A pair of loudspeaker has been placed at each corner of this screen. The man's gestures generate violent sounds and the screen moves accordingly. The man appears to be trapped in a digital reality. Whether it is illusion or delusion, QQ seems to be living in a Matrix world: a prisoner of his own imagination who attracts attention by making an infernal din.

Ni Haifeng (1964, Zhoushan) exhibited a miniature reality rather than a digital one. He showed two recordings of the Dutch miniature city of Madurodam that were projected next to each other. Madurodam was founded in 1952 by Mr. and Mrs. Maduro of Willemstad, Curacao. They were seeking a monument for their only son George who died of typhus in February 1945 in the concentration camp Dachau. George was posthumously awarded the *Militaire Willemsorde* for his actions during the first days of the war. Hence, George Maduro was a Dutch national hero from the colonies and Madurodam was to become his anthropological monument for the suffering that his enforced fatherland had caused him.

For NiHaifeng, this particular history and the country's depicted miniaturisation are interesting data for the analysis of the complexity of present realities and histories. He views Madurodam as a form of exotic, Dutch nationalism that could be compared with a representation of a Beijing street in an ethnological museum. This introverted exoticism displays such oddities as the miniature skid course for drivers, which has been filmed by NiHaifeng. The result is an alienating image of a car that constantly makes the same skid. There is also the rotating, miniature China Airlines plane at Schiphol Airport, a wink in the direction of the Chinese public.

Ni enlarges this miniaturised reality with the film's projection. The viewer does not immediately realise that this is a created reality. But the pipe is not the pipe. This is a recording filmed by a Chinese artist of the 'image' of the Netherlands as created by Dutch people from overseas territories. The Dutch national anthem, which is played at Madurodam by pushing a quarter into a machine, can be heard in the background.

Imagine History
Wang Jianwei observes his own Chinese history. He has incorporated memories of the Communist era, which include existing film footage, into his installation *Is He a Traitor?*. Here, he uses images from the Russian film *Lenin in 1918*, which applauded the Bolshevik Revolution and was enormously popular in China. Directed by Mikhail Romm, it was a sequel to his successful film *Lenin in October* (1937). Both films deal with a dictatorial, Communist film reality that was extremely frightening and threatening for many of the inhabitants of Russia. The installation's title *Is He a Traitor?* symbolises the emotions of that time when people betrayed each other and were murdered or imprisoned.
Short fragments are endlessly repeated as some of the images become vaguer, while others become sharper and brighter. The original soundtrack is mixed with other sounds to constitute a sonic narra-

tive that reinterprets history according to the artist's own memories of the film and of the communist era. This sound gradually desynchronizes and resynchronizes with the images during the repetition. This multi-media installation consists of video images, a soundtrack and a photo on a light box. It is located in a dark space that resembles a cinema and is illuminated only by the light box and the projectors. A portrait of the 'traitor' and the film's famous sentence are on the light box. The entire installation is enveloped by the thunderous sounds of revolutionary rhetoric. The pride of historical reality has been superseded by history itself.

Last Words by Zhang Peili (1957, Hangzhou) also plays with historical depiction and focuses on the Chinese heroism of the films of the 1950s and '60s, which were made during the Cultural Revolution. Zhang uses death scenes from these old, patriotic films and plays them both forwards and backwards. He then places both sequences opposite each other so that the hero dies and is simultaneously resurrected. After all, these heroes of the Revolution were immortal. They are a part of the collective memory of the People's Republic of China. As such they cannot be erased even if they are fantasy figures and symbolise the Cultural Revolution with all its difficulties. Yet these endless death scenes and resurrections are simply hilarious. The work shows the absurdity of ideological and dramatic political messages.

Synthetic Reality in Context 2
The Synthetic Realities exhibition is a part of a global trend towards Chinese contemporary art. Here, examples include the 1996 *Reckoning with the Past, Contemporary Chinese Painting exhibition* at the Fruitmarket Gallery in Edinburgh, the 1997 *Another Long March, Chinese Conceptual and Installation Art in the Nineties* show in the Dutch city of Breda, the Venice Biennale's extensive attention for Chinese contemporary art in 2001, and Hou Hanru's 2002 *Asian Vibe* exhibition at the Espai d'Art Contemporain in Castello, Spain. *Alors, la Chine?*, a major retrospective of current cultural expression in China, took place at the Centre Pompidou in Paris as recently as 2003. In addition, a number of shows of modern Chinese art are currently touring Europe, Asia and Australia.

Synthetic Realities was particularly innovative for its focus on digital media and video art. The fact that it was held in Beijing was also daring. Moreover, it was an artists' initiative, which emphasises just how important it was for the artists to ensure that this work, which is mostly shown outside of China, could now be shown in China itself.

The exhibition stimulated Chinese artists to work with video and the digital media. It also reinforced the local Beijing art scene and contributed to the debate about art and the meaning of art in society. A changing reality is emerging in China. The artists of *Synthetic Realities* analyse, elucidate and distort this current reality, and this expresses the desire for an open society where these kinds of initiatives can take place with increasing frequency. These are not dramatic Last Words, such as those of the dying film heroes, rather they are the positive and energetic statements of an artistic future to come.

"Synthetic Reality":A Historical Note

Pi Li

Today, it is difficult to image back a decade and a half ago, when video art made its first appearance in China, just what it signified. Although video art was certainly an imported medium, its emergence in China was not a mere case of following in the footsteps of the West. It could only have been born under a certain state of affairs, after certain cultural preconditions had been met. To put it more concretely, Chinese video art was not simply the product of a search for artistic language, but a phenomenon tinged with ideology and an opposition to cultural imperialism that western observers might be hard pressed to comprehend.

Long before the appearance of video art in 1990, Chinese artists were well aware of the danger of their art being manipulated by politics. But with the advent of cynical realism and political pop, there arose new dangers: the lure of commercial incentives and the peril of being manipulated by western cultural neocolonialism. Both dangers had their roots in old-fashioned mediums and methodologies. This was the background against which young Chinese artists of the time began to experiment with video art. They were searching for a new medium that could resist commercialism by western galleries, while at the same time provide a contrast to more official mainstream art. Video art was a medium that allowed for the expression of individual feelings and language, and it was also easy to use, disseminate and exchange. Under these circumstances, video art became their medium of choice.

For these young artists, the element of time in video made it a more profound viewing experience than other more traditional mediums. It had an experiential force that transcended language, an experienced meaning that words alone could not exhaust. Unlike realist painting, video art was something that had to be experienced within a certain time frame. In addition, interactive video installations invited viewers to physically participate in the process of visual appreciation. It is interesting to note that the more profound implications of the Chinese translation of the term video art ("luxiang yishu"). The second character "xiang" connotes °∞reflect". Perhaps this is one reason Chinese artists chose video as a medium, for video art seemed to evoke a deeper experiential response than traditional painting, one more suited to the fundamental nature of art itself.

Against this backdrop, the first few experimental video artists found themselves face to face with a medium in which images intersected with human psychology and visual experience. They hoped to employ the newfound medium in an effort to change the face of contemporary Chinese art, a visage distorted by years of political and ideological conflict. Zhu Jia and Zhang Peili were two early and contemporaneous pioneers of Chinese video art. In 1991, Zhang Peili completed his first video piece, a work in which he stressed the difference between video art and television programs designed for a mass audience. So committed was he to highlighting this contrast that he eschewed any and all conventional television or film techniques, sound effects and anything even remotely resembling a TV screen. This tendency is even more marked in Zhang's well-known later work "Uncertain Pleasure" (1994). At about this time, Beijing-based artist Zhu Jia was attempting to link video and physical experience by attaching a camcorder to the moving wheel of a tricycle. He dubbed the result, a seemingly endless rotation of images, "Forever". These were China's earliest works of video art, a fact not to be overlooked in our retrospective of this period of history. Both Zhang Peili and Zhu Jia took physical motion as the starting point for their video art. Li Yongbin did something similar, although the difference is that he turned his own body and physical experience into an indispensable element in his artwork, something to be inspected and examined within a certain video time frame. The level of extreme and practiced self awareness in these video works of art causes us, as observers, to feel both anxious and uneasy.

From another standpoint, the emergence of video art in China can be considered the result of a fundamental reassessment of international video art prior to 1990. For this reason, Chinese artists often referred to so-called "classic" video art as "standard video art" or even "insipid tradition". Chinese artists began to pay more attention to the possibilities of video technology and the aesthetic value it afforded. For them, "standard" western video art had become a canon that threatened to overlook new developments, more affordable equipment and recent technological leaps in video. The aesthetic dullness of early western video art can be blamed partly on its anti-establishment mentality and partly on the financial and technological limitations of its time. It would be foolish to neglect the cultural context and technological limitations of early video art and take its dullness as some sort of standard or inherited style, for this provides no aesthetic value whatsoever. Chinese video artists understood this, and began to realize that cravenly following the established standards of western video art would cause them to lose whatever inherent value they already possessed. This realization led Chinese video artists to experiment with narrative, interactivity and other techniques.

Narrative was born of a questioning of traditional video art. New video techniques now enabled video art to share the fruits of film aesthetics—classic methods of film chronology proved to be as applicable to video art as they were to movies. Moreover, digital technology made this chronology vastly more flexible. Digital special effects yielded more and better ways to weave together narrative threads, vastly enriching cinematic language. And the advent of three dimensional animation had made it possible to turn even the most fantastic idea into a visual reality. All of the above opened up a whole new world of possibilities for Chinese video artists. One influential artist who remained well aware of the possibilities of self-written and produced works accessible to a common audience was Chinese video artist Wang Jianwei. In Wang's video installation piece "Connection", he projected two videos running simultaneously on opposite walls of a hallway. On one wall was a montage of violent and sexual scenes from pirated copies of overseas films he had spliced together to create a "new cinema". Juxtaposed on the other wall were scenes of eight Chinese families watching television. Wang used the simplest techniques, most anathema to film professionals, to illuminate our cultural condition. In doing so, he challenged not only the "standard video art" but also the conventional aesthetics of film. Perhaps the most significant aspect of his work is his consistent use of convenient, low cost digital technology to create a °∞new narrative°± to challenge old narratives dominated by commerce and politics.

Interactivity grew out of suspicions about the very nature of video art itself: Would video art find itself engulfed by cinematic aesthetics and insipid tradition? What if any aesthetic value, aside from improved image quality and convenience, did digital technology have to offer? In the context of this questioning, video installation art began to attract more attention from artists as a "here and now" artistic medium. Video installation possessed the distinctive attributes of both video and installation art, and yet it was much more than the sum of the two parts. The use of multiple video monitors broadcasting a variety of video channels or projected images distributed across a certain structure could create a more vivid three dimensional dramatic format. Chinese video art developed into two distinct types of video installation art: one focused on intrinsic knowledge and one focused on intrinsic experience.

Video installations that stress intrinsic knowledge tend to take place in a specific setting, and may employ physical "props" to create a semantic connection with the video images. Meaning is produced by the images themselves, and through the use of props to help develop or advance the overall theme. "Multiple Lies", a recent work by photographer and installation artist Ni Haifeng, was an interface between photos and video that transformed semantic meaning by relying heavily on the intellectual judgment of the observer. Wang Gongxin did something similar in his video installation "Baby Talk", in which images of a family playing with a baby were projected onto a cradle filled with milk. As the milk flowed down a drain installed in the bottom of the cradle, it appeared to flow into the "mouth" of the image, before being circulated back into the cradle.

Video installations that stress intrinsic experience often take into account the physical movement of the observer. Chen Shaoxing's early video installation piece "Eye-Rectifier" and Shi Yong's "Restricted Area" were two such works designed to incorporate audience movement into the artwork itself. Based on the concept of "anthropo-engineering", these video installations were timed to coincide with the arrival of the observer either at a set location or by a pre-designated route. The presence of the observer was a precondition that played an integral part in the structure and setting of the artwork. The world of phenomena that arose from the passage of each visitor signaled not extrinsic knowledge but an awakening of intrinsic experience.

Video installation brought interactivity to the forefront of the artistic agenda. Artists pursued interactivity as a means of defining the true potential of video art, but it proved to be a bitter pill. The more they quested after interactivity, the more they grew to doubt the validity of video art and the space it could provide. For this reason, many artists began to seek interactive methods beyond video installation art. Artists favoring more experiential art began to abandon video in favor of newer technologies, which led to the appearance of more technologically rigorous and design-focused interactive multimedia art. Artists favoring knowledge-based art, on the other hand, sought to reach new levels of face to face and psychological interaction through the destruction of media itself.

In examining the development of video art in China, we can see that a new era is approaching. Western video art was born of rebellion against the system, whereas Chinese video art grew out of an interest in new forms of media. After 1968, the involvement of private foundations in the western art world served to greatly enhance the professionalism of video art. Over the past twenty years, western video art has steadily severed its ties with film, television and photography, and moved into art museum territory. This in turn has led to a synthesis between video and installation art. Over time, video art turned away from its role as info-culture critic and began to synthesize different strains of social thought, which won it a new-found legitimacy. Video art has a duty to critique our information culture, but this is not by any means its only duty. Contemporary art, with its emphasis on individuality and craftsmanship, is by its very nature ill-suited to hold any real dialogue with the commercialized mass media, much less act as its driving force. The relationship between the mass media and video art, particularly as it was practiced prior to 1968, is similar to that of a flyswatter and a particularly stubborn fly. Now Chinese artists, like their international contemporaries, have begun to realize that the only place they will ever find their own territory and style is in a place well beyond the reach of the authority of mass media.

The quest for interactivity is the perennial dream of contemporary art. But as we have seen, many Chinese and international pioneers of video art lost their faith in video art as a medium and turned instead to multimedia art, with its greater technological and design potential. Though blind resistance to the phenomenon of multimedia art would be every bit as futile and absurd as blind faith in the medium, the present reality of Chinese video art does bring with it certain realizations. By moving away from info-culture criticism and toward synthesis, video art gained a new legitimacy. Is it perhaps time for video art to resynthesize and re-establish its early connections with film, television, photography and other areas in order to salvage its relevance? For Chinese video art, it may be necessary to decide once and for all whether video should be considered a form of media or a form of culture. In one direction lies evolution; in the other, pluralism. It is a decision that could lead to two very different outcomes.

Chen Shaoxiong

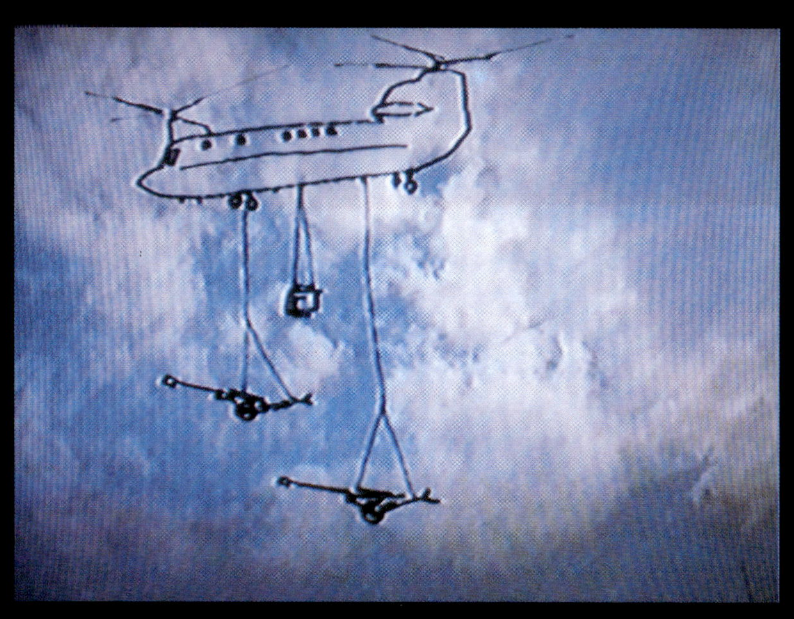

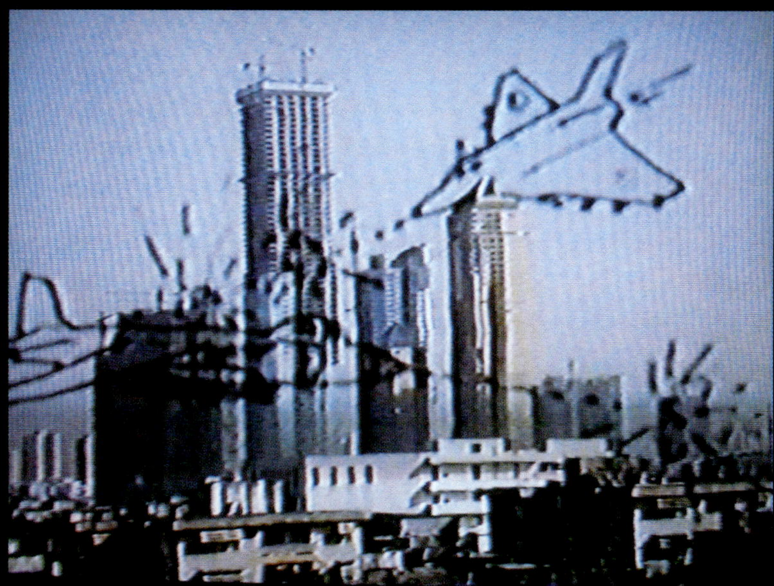

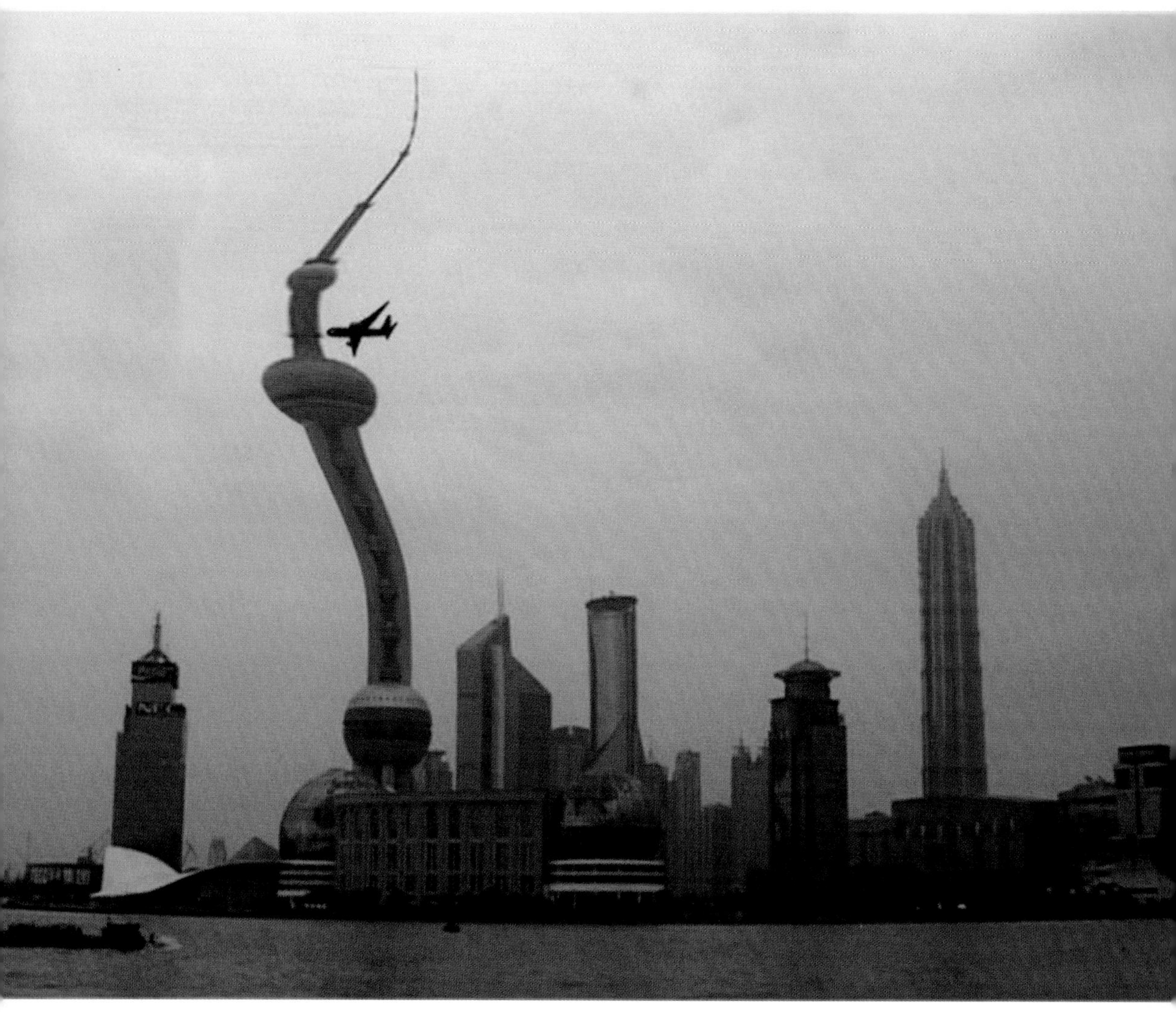

Windows 2002

Chen Shaoxiong, 2002

video installation, single channel, 4 minutes, dimensions variable, installation at EMAC BeijingChina, 2002

video still

The video shows skyscrapers taking on odd shapes in order to dodge airplanes and missiles.

视窗 2002

陈绍雄 2002

可变尺寸单视频录像装置，4分钟，远洋艺术中心，北京，中国

这部录像显现的是各种各样经过数码处理的都市风景，每一个场景中都有一座正在躲避飞机和导弹的柔软灵活的摩天大楼。

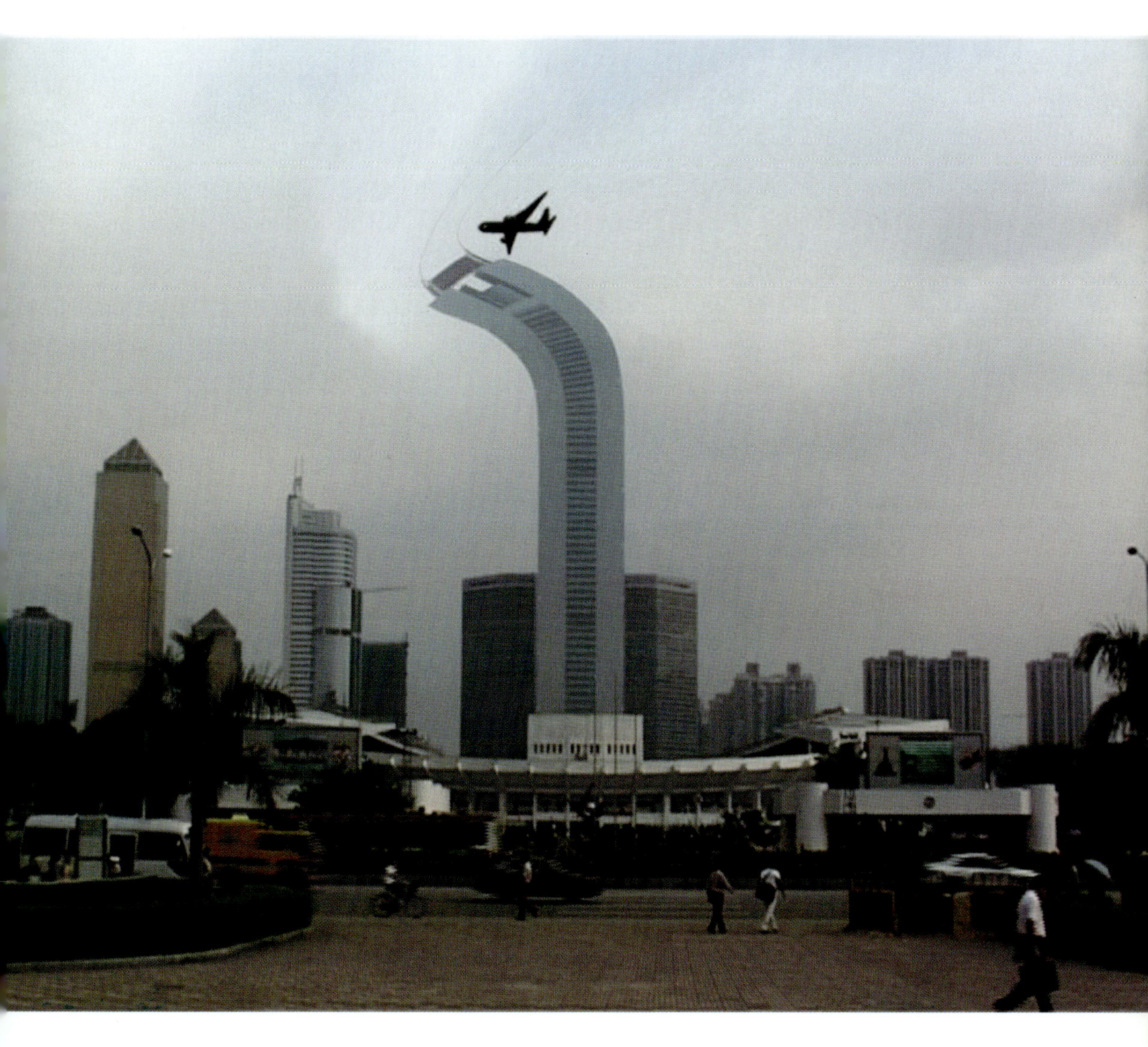

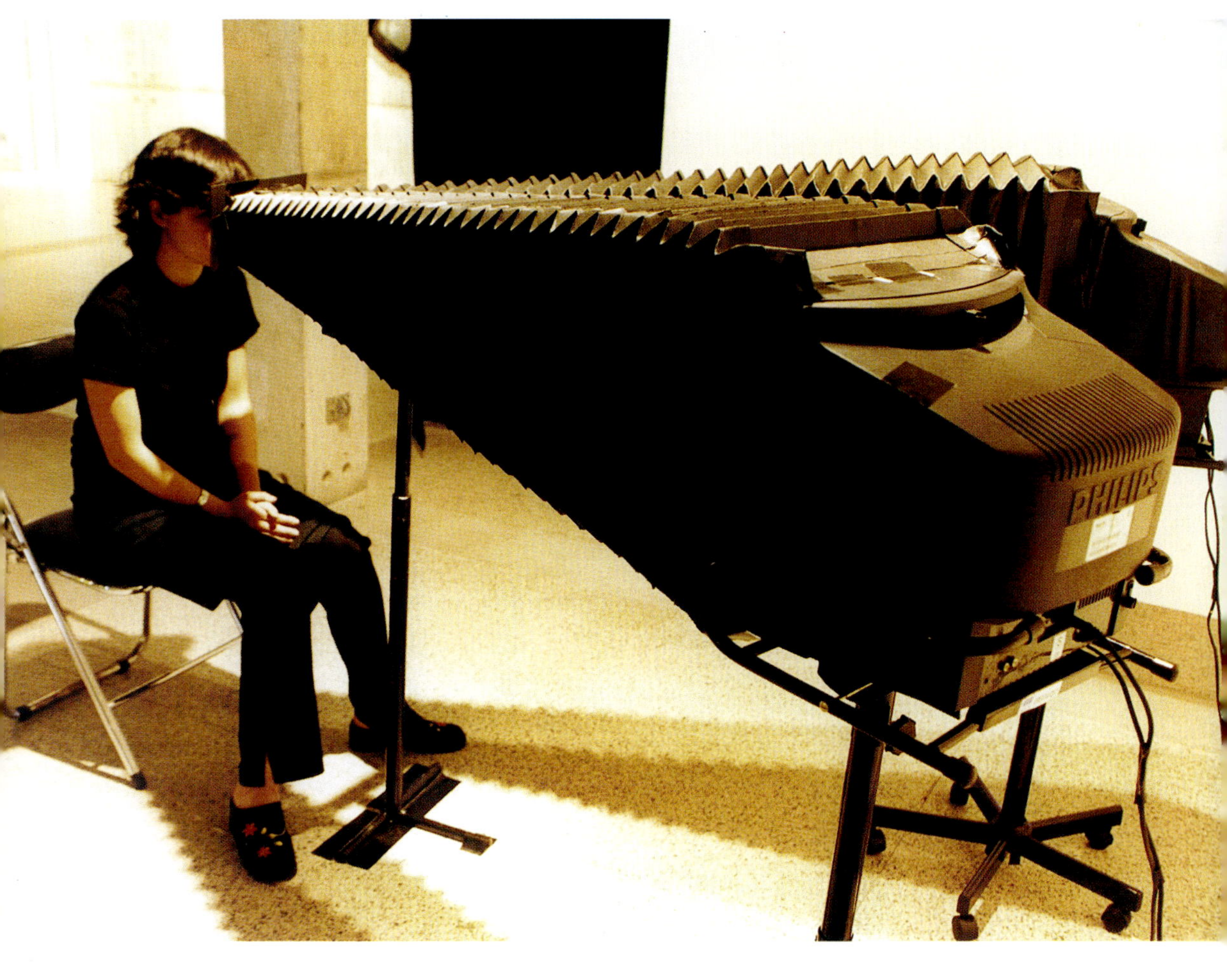

Eye Rectifier-III

Chen Shaoxiong, 1996

video installation

视力矫正器 −3

陈绍雄 1996

录像装置

Hero

Chen Shaoxiong, 2001

video, single channel, 10 minutes

video still

In a Hollywood style, the artist stars in the film as a hero fighting in a city. With a fully programmed toy gun, he fights invisible enemies in various settings, such as in a subway station, on the streets and in an elevator.

英雄

陈绍雄 2001

单视频录像，10分钟

录像照片

这部录像戏仿好莱坞风格的打斗片。艺术家本人在这部片子中扮演一个与城市战斗的英雄。他用一支多功能玩具枪在城市的各个角落与虚构的敌人战斗。

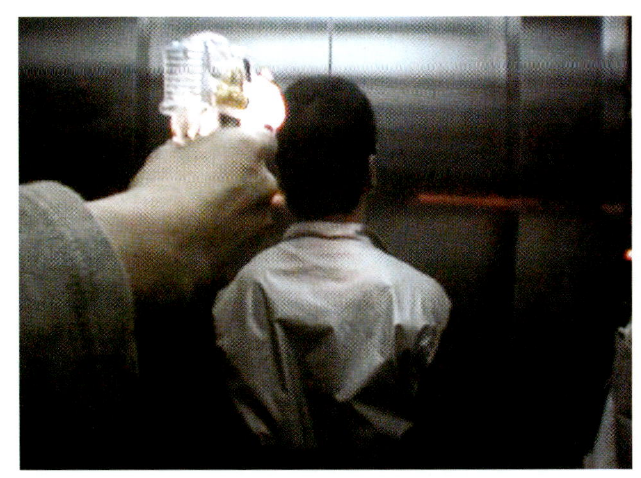

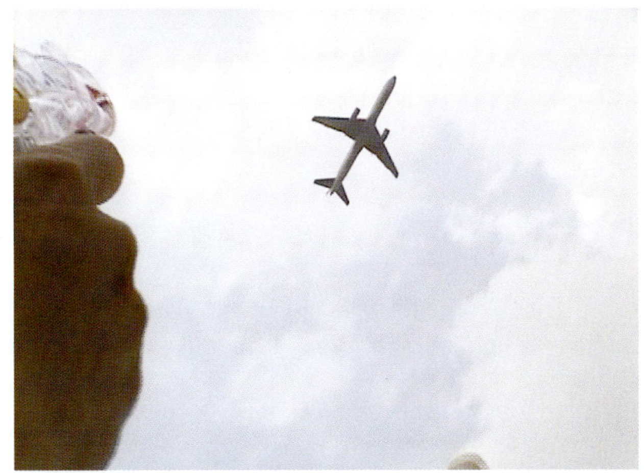

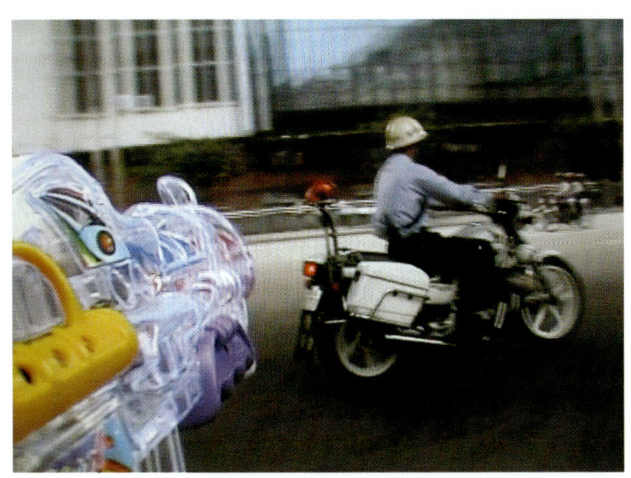

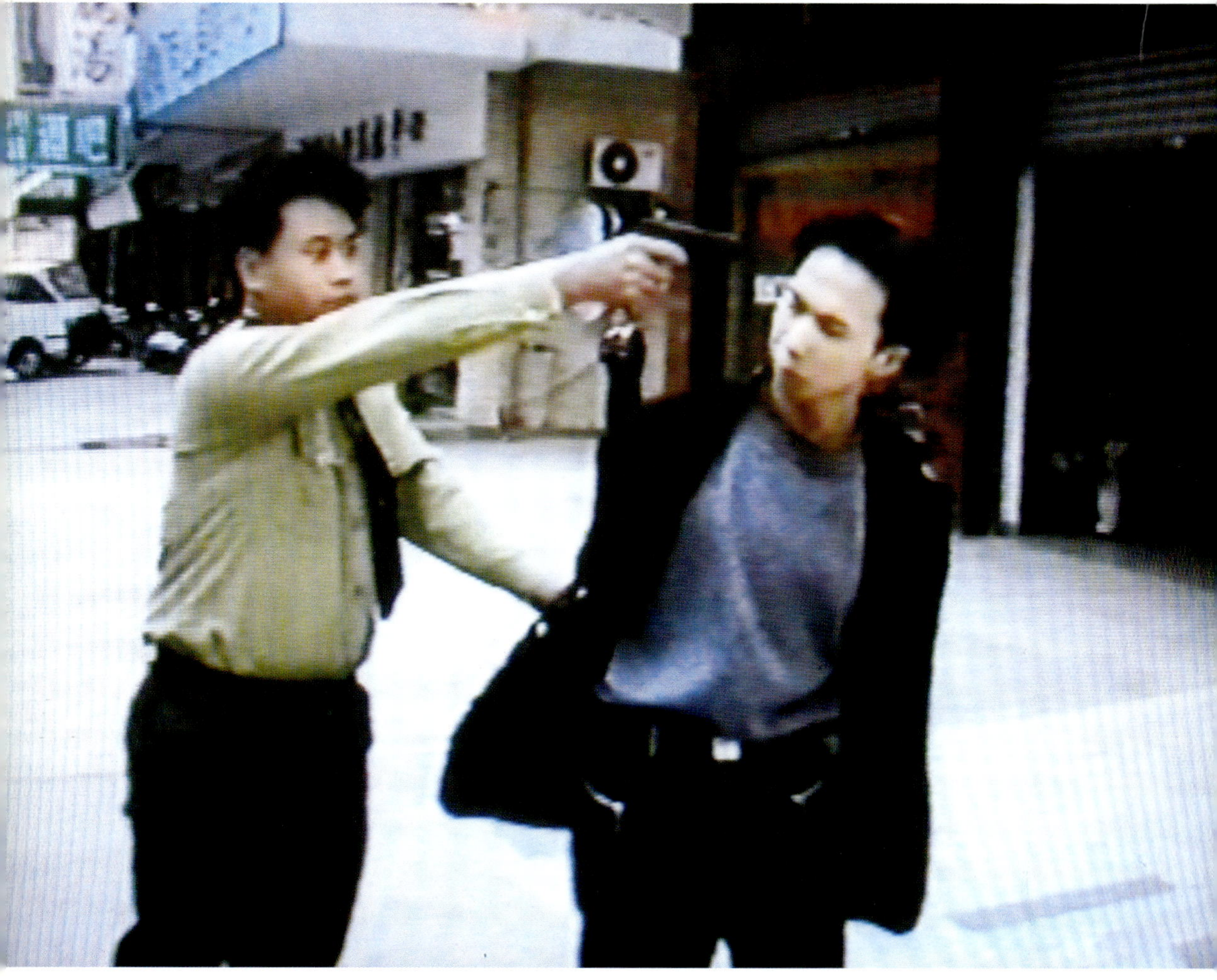

The Policeman and the Thief

Chen Shaoxiong, 1997

video, single channel, 8 minutes, video still

The film consists of three components: two mirror-imaged narratives and the film title in the middle of the timeline. The first part of the film shows a policeman catching, interrogating and executing a thief. The last part shows the same story but with the actors' roles switched - the "policeman" becomes a thief and the "thief" a policeman.

警察与小偷

陈绍雄 1997

单视频录像，8分钟

录像照片

这一录像由三个元素构成：两个分别在开始与结尾处的镜像叙事和位于中间处的片头、片尾字幕。影片的前半部分叙述的是一个警察抓获、审讯和枪决一个小偷。字幕后，警察与小偷互换角色上演同样的剧情。

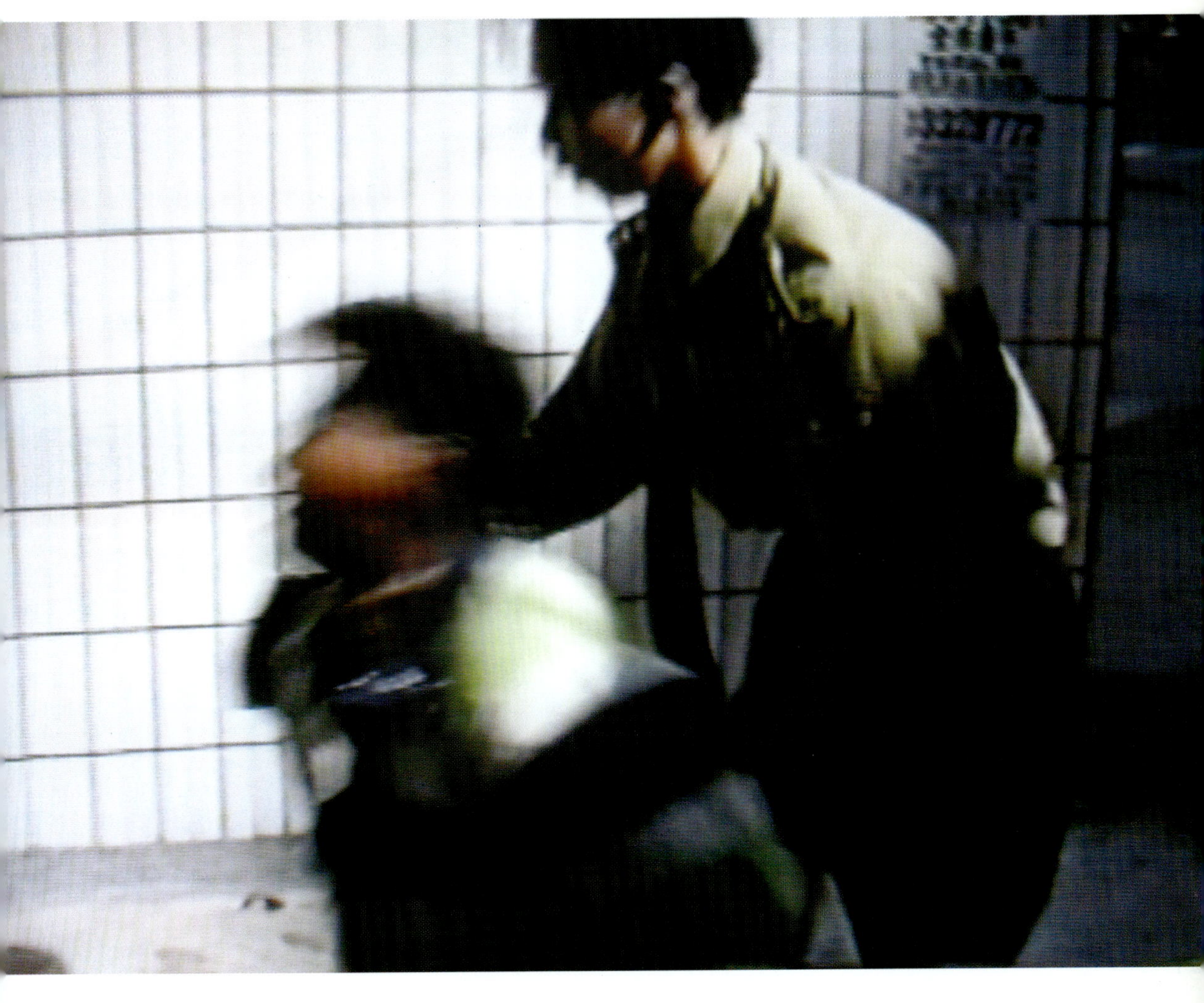

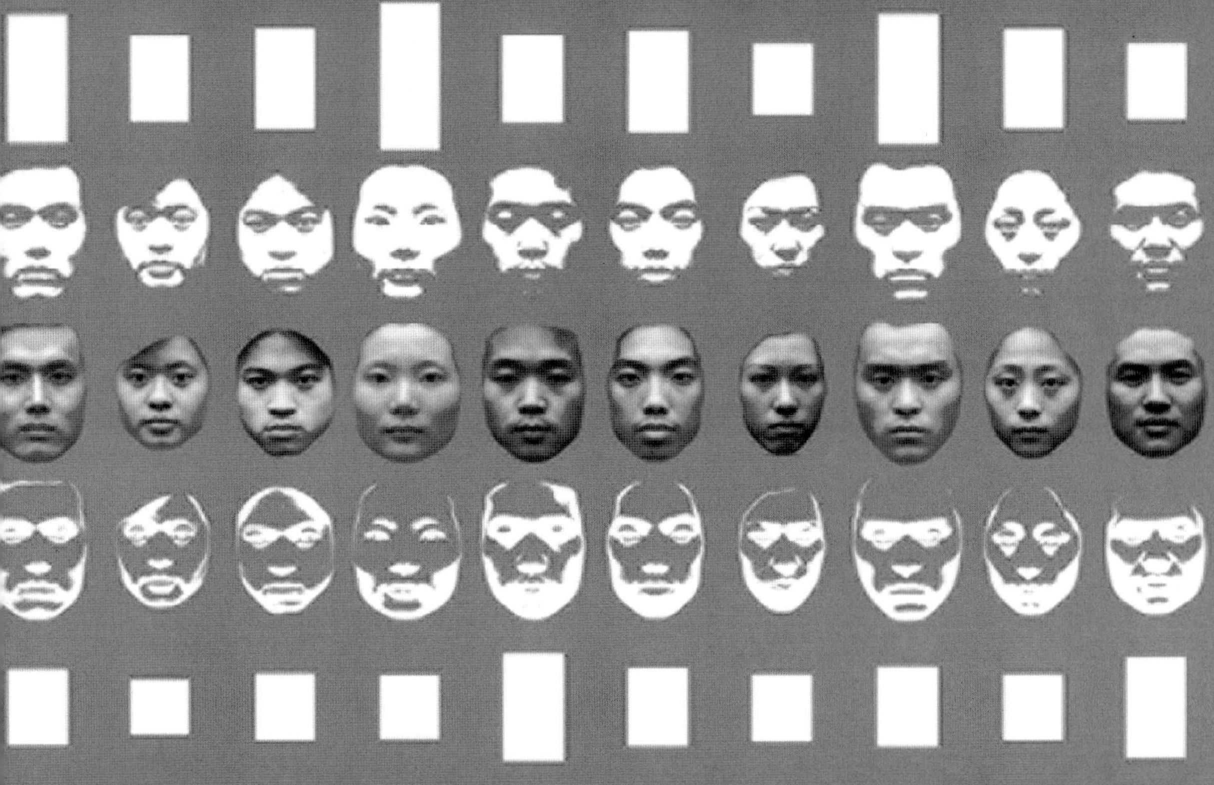

光明的一面和黑暗的一面 10 号
耿建翌，1999—2001
照片，120 × 390（厘米）

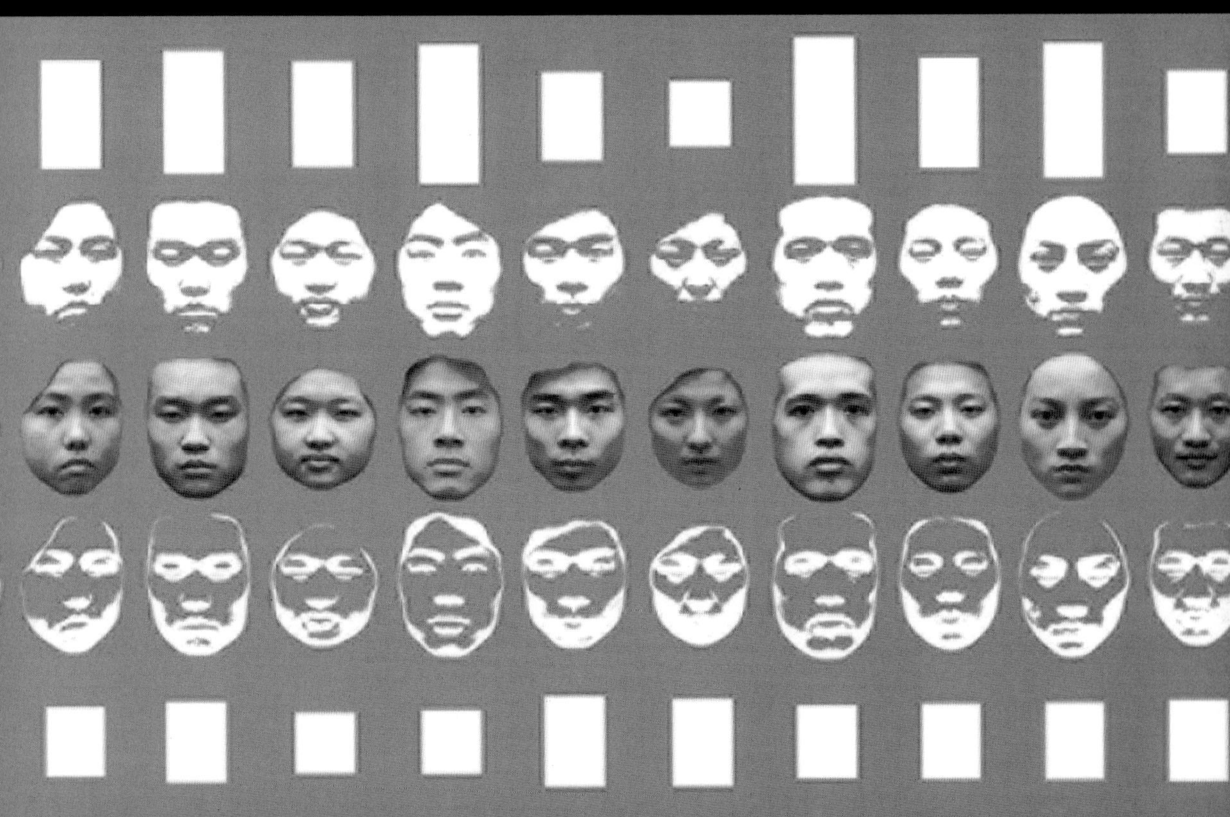

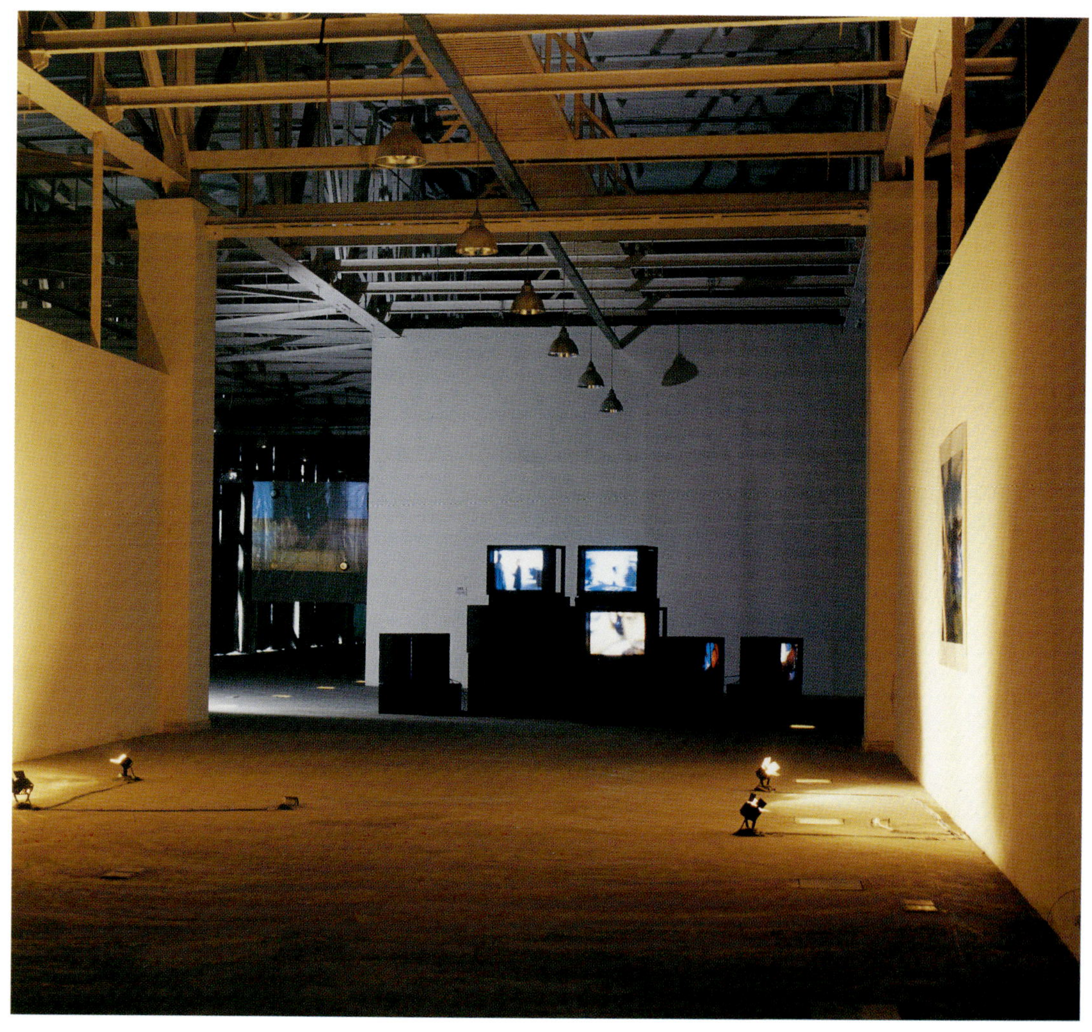

Related to 'Synthetic Reality'

Geng Jianyi, 2002

9 monitors, 9 video channels, dimensions variable

installation at EMAC, Beijing (China), 2002

The work consists of 9 video portraits of the 9 participating artists of the
exhibition. The work reveals the processes of artistic creation and exhibition
making that are usually hidden to the public.

有关"合成现实"

耿建翌，2002

9视频录像装置，监视器，尺寸可变，远洋艺术中心，北京，中国，
2002

这部作品包含9个录像肖像，记录9位参展艺术家的生活与工作。该作品揭示
了艺术创作以及展览制作过程中的幕后故事.

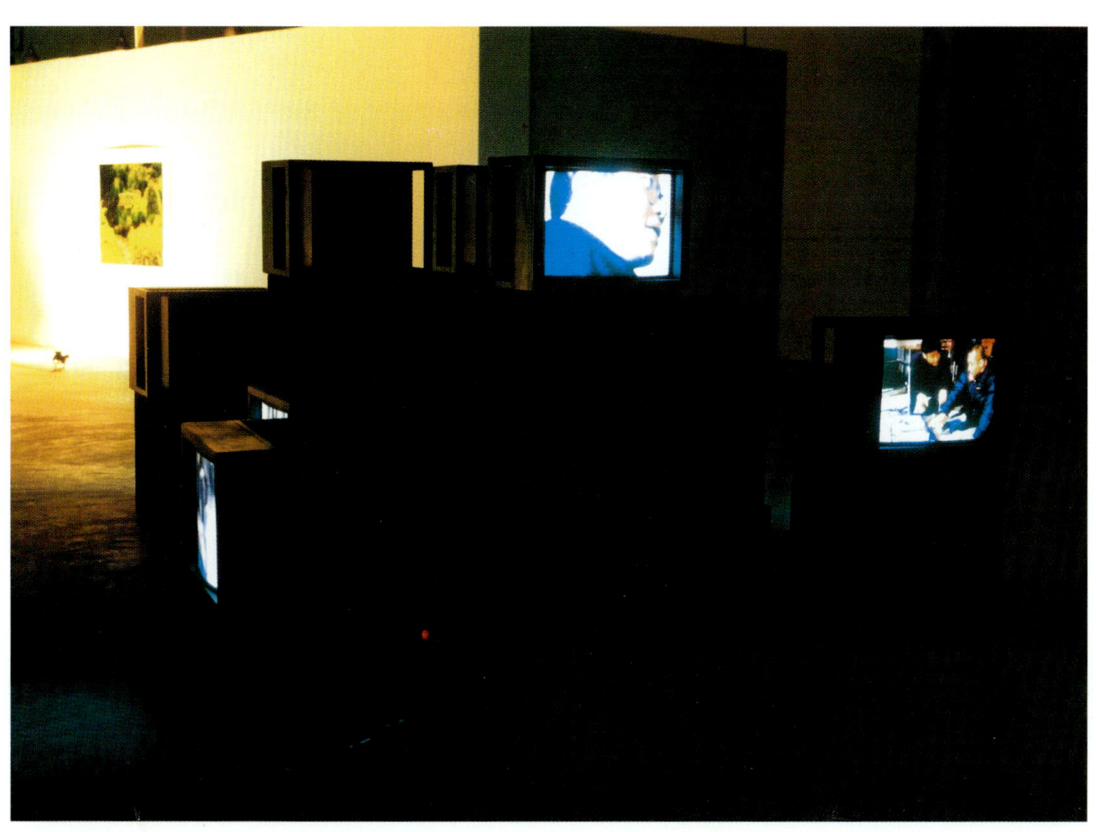

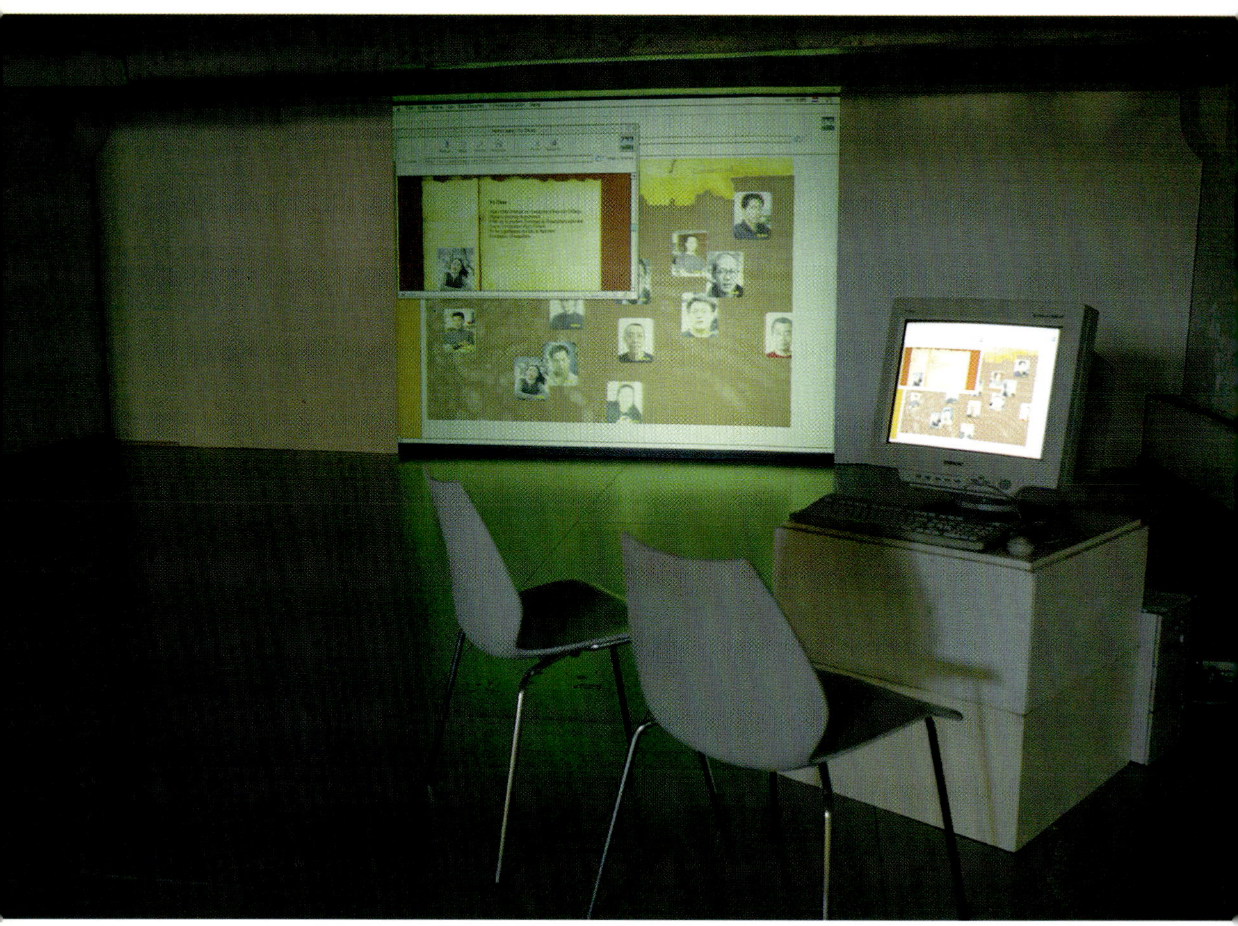

Connected

Geng Jianyi, 2001

interactive installation, website, data projection, dimensions variable, installation at EMAC, Beijing (China), 2002
The website investigates the past and the present state of the Dutch VOC. The work is an ongoing process that connects those who are related to the trade history.

有牵连

耿建翌，2001

互动网页装置，电脑，投影，空间可变，远洋艺术中心，北京，中国，2002
这个网站有关荷兰东印度公司的过去与现在。艺术家的意图是，通过这一处于不断发展中的作品，使每一个与这一段特殊历史有关的
人联系起来。

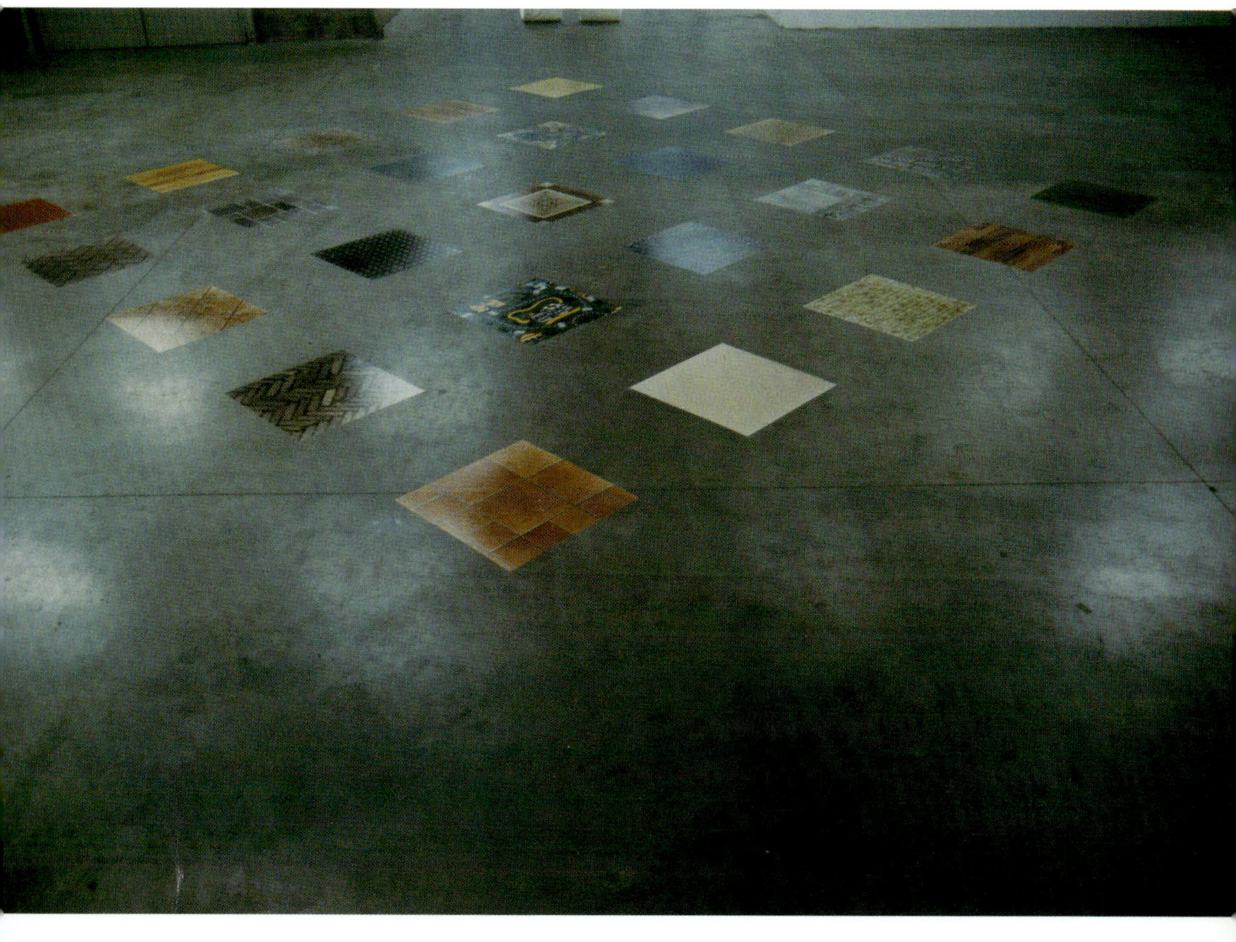

Floor

Geng Jianyi, 1997
installation, 25 photographs from 25 locations, 25 perplex plates,
80cm x 80cm each, ca.720cm x 720cm.

地板

耿建翌，1997
装置，25 张不同地点的照片（80x80／每张），25 张有机玻璃，720x720 厘米

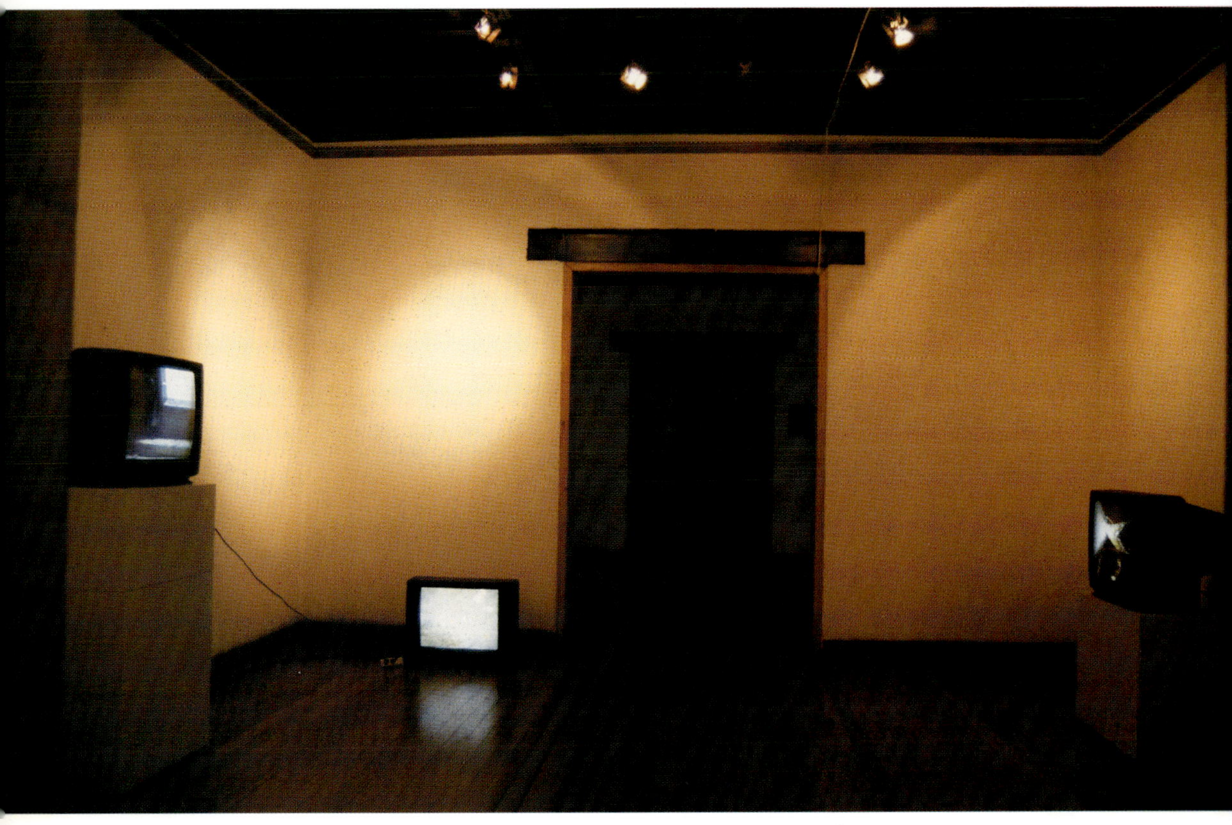

The Complete World

Geng Jianyi, 1996

video installation, 3 channels

*Four monitors respectively show a windowsill, a tabletop,
a doorframe and part of the floor. At various intervals, a
fly enters the images, and when the fly disappears from the
scenes, the viewer hears the sound of the fly echoing
through the space.*

完整的世界

耿建翌，1996

3 视频录像装置

四个监视器分别展示了窗框、门框、桌面和地板。一只苍蝇
相继飞入这四个画面。当苍蝇飞出所有画面时，观众听到苍
蝇的嗡嗡声。

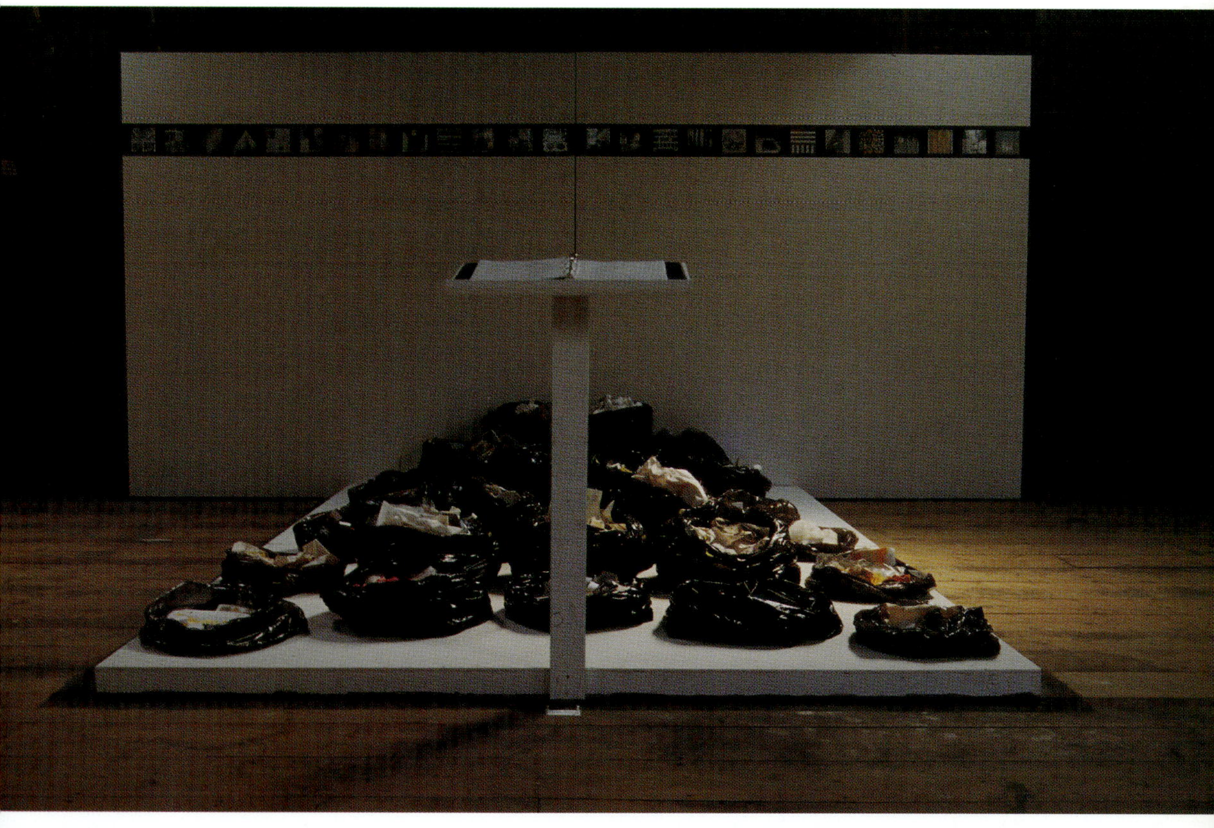

Choice

Geng Jianyi, 1996
installation, various materials, rubbish bag,
photograph,dimensions variable
*The rubbish bags contain various art materials that
are discarded by artists in an artist in residence
program. The photographs show the final works of
the artists.*

选择

耿建翌，1996
装置，诸种物体，垃圾袋，照片，可变尺寸
垃圾袋里装有从不同的艺术家们手里搜集来的艺术材
料，照片显示的则是这些艺术家创作的最后结果。

Li Yongbin

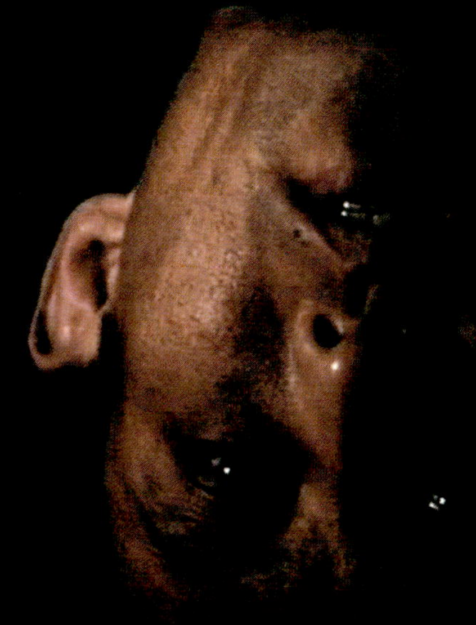

Face-II

Li Yongbin, 1996-1997

video, single channel, 36 minutes

The images depict the artist's own face reflected in a bowl of black ink. The movement of the fluid transforms the face into various distorted figures.

脸—2

李永斌 1996–1997

单视频录像，36分钟

这个录像纪录了艺术家本人的脸倒影在黑墨之中，
液体的无规则运动把他的脸扭曲成各种怪异的形状。

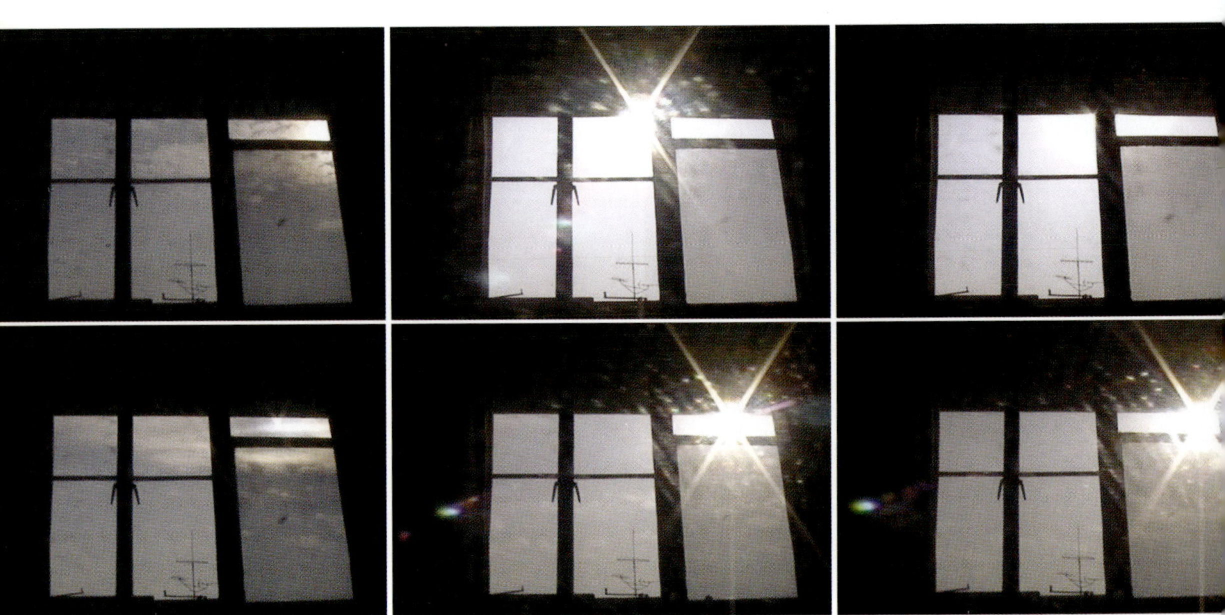

The Sun

Li Yongbin, 2002

video installation, single channel, soundtrack, 60 minutesloop, video still
The work consists of a one-hour video loop of a window behind which the winter sun is passing. This lethargic image is accompanied by a piece by Bach that is played at 50% of the normal speed.

太阳

李永斌，2002

单视频录像，六十分钟

这个作品由一个60分钟的循环录像构成，录像拍摄的内容是冬日里太阳穿过窗外的天空的过程。与之相伴的是一首巴赫的音乐，节奏被缓慢到原音乐的一半。

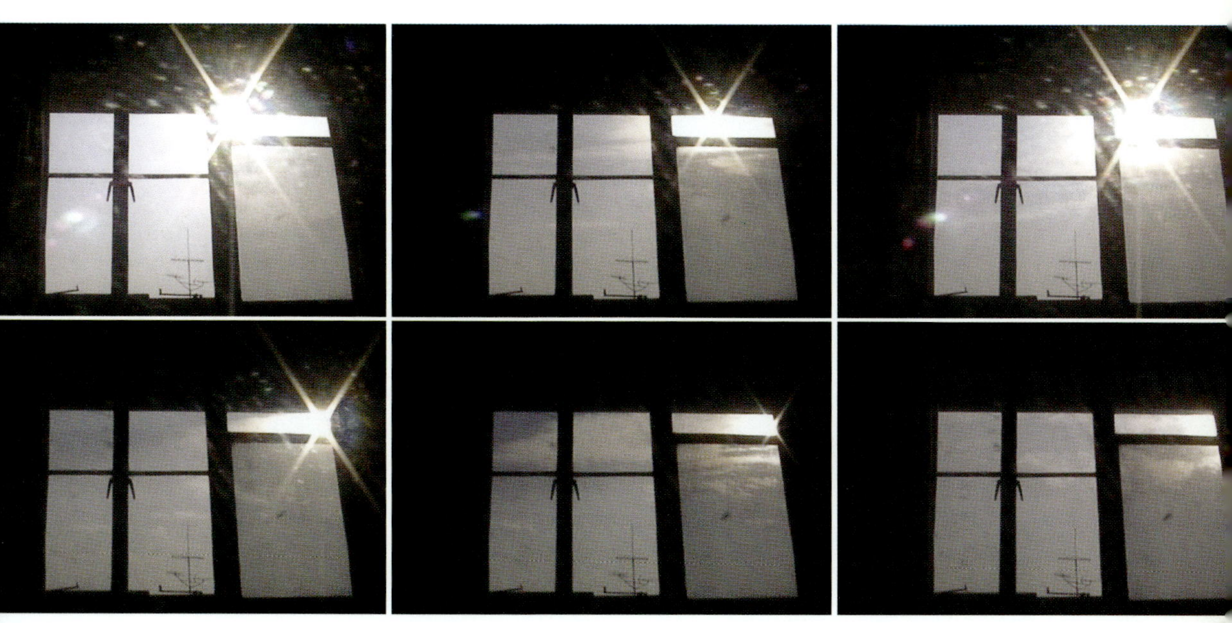

Face-IV

Li Yongbin, 1998

video, single channel, 60 minutes, loop, video still

The video shows the image of the artist's face reflected on a windowpane against a cityscape at the moment of sunset. As noght falls, the cityscape gradually disappears from the superimposed images.

脸—4

李永斌，1998

单视频录像，六十分钟 Face-IV

该录像记录了照映在窗户上的艺术家的面孔，与窗外黄昏时分的城市风景相重叠。随着夜暮降临，城市风景逐渐从这一重叠影像中消失。

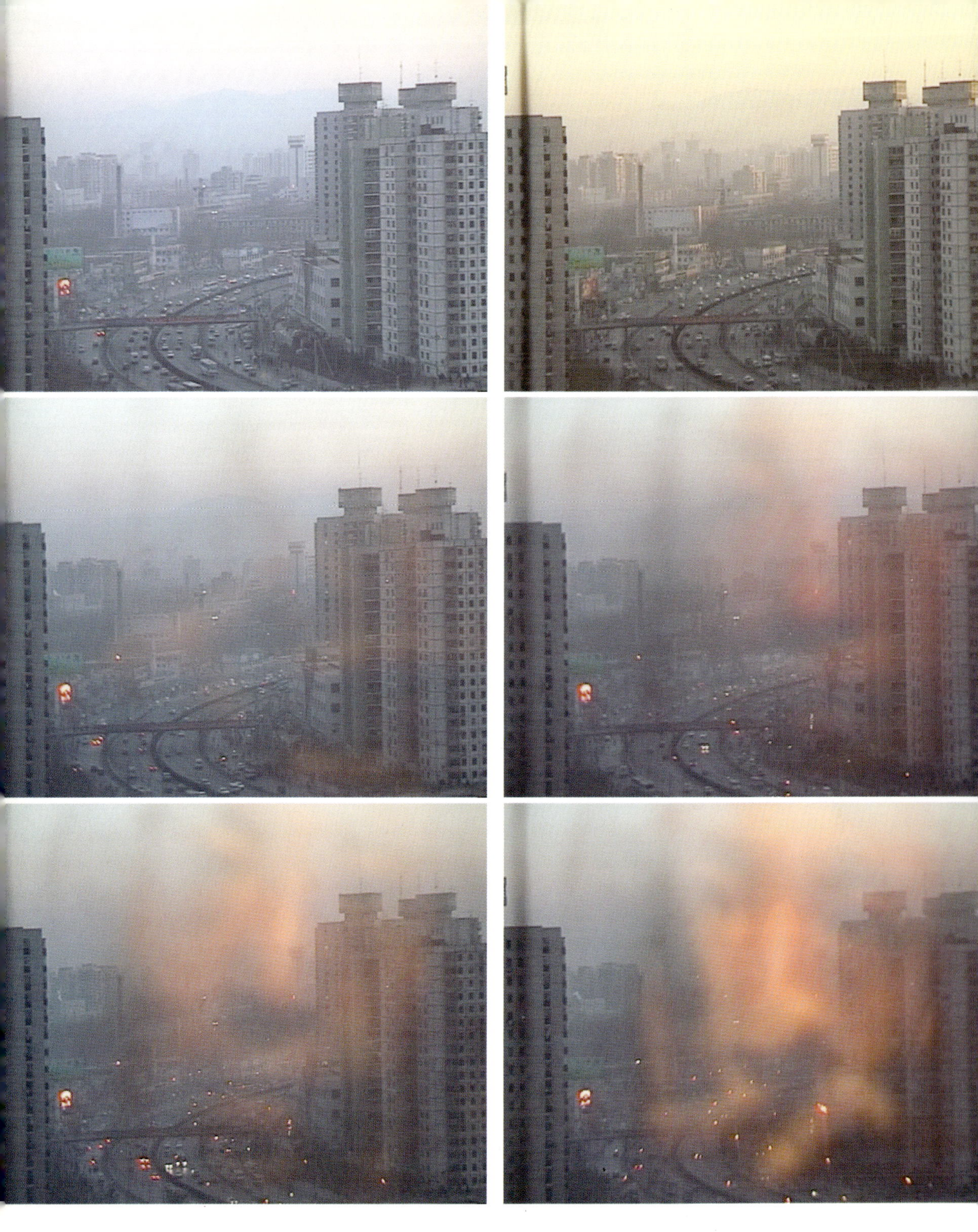

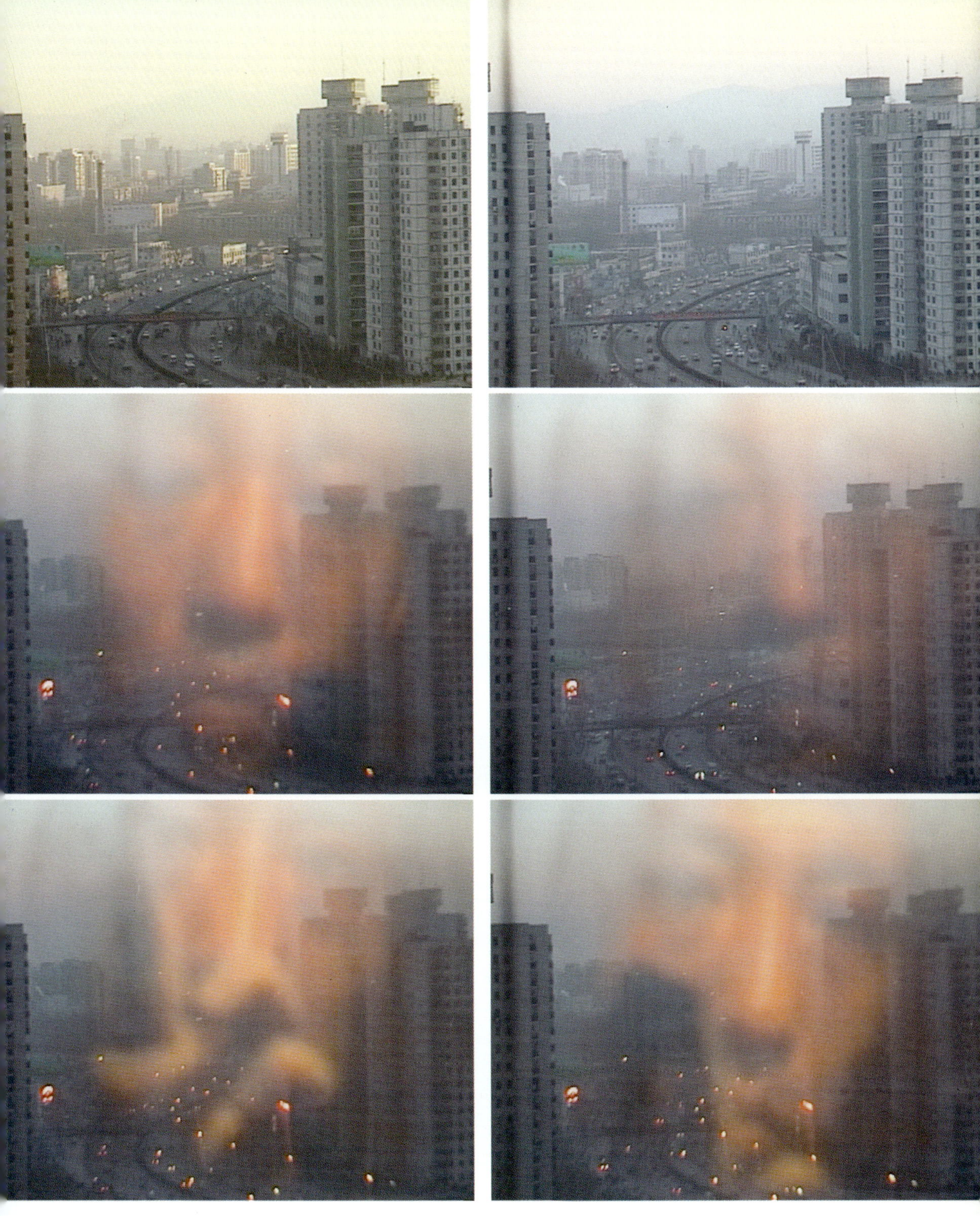

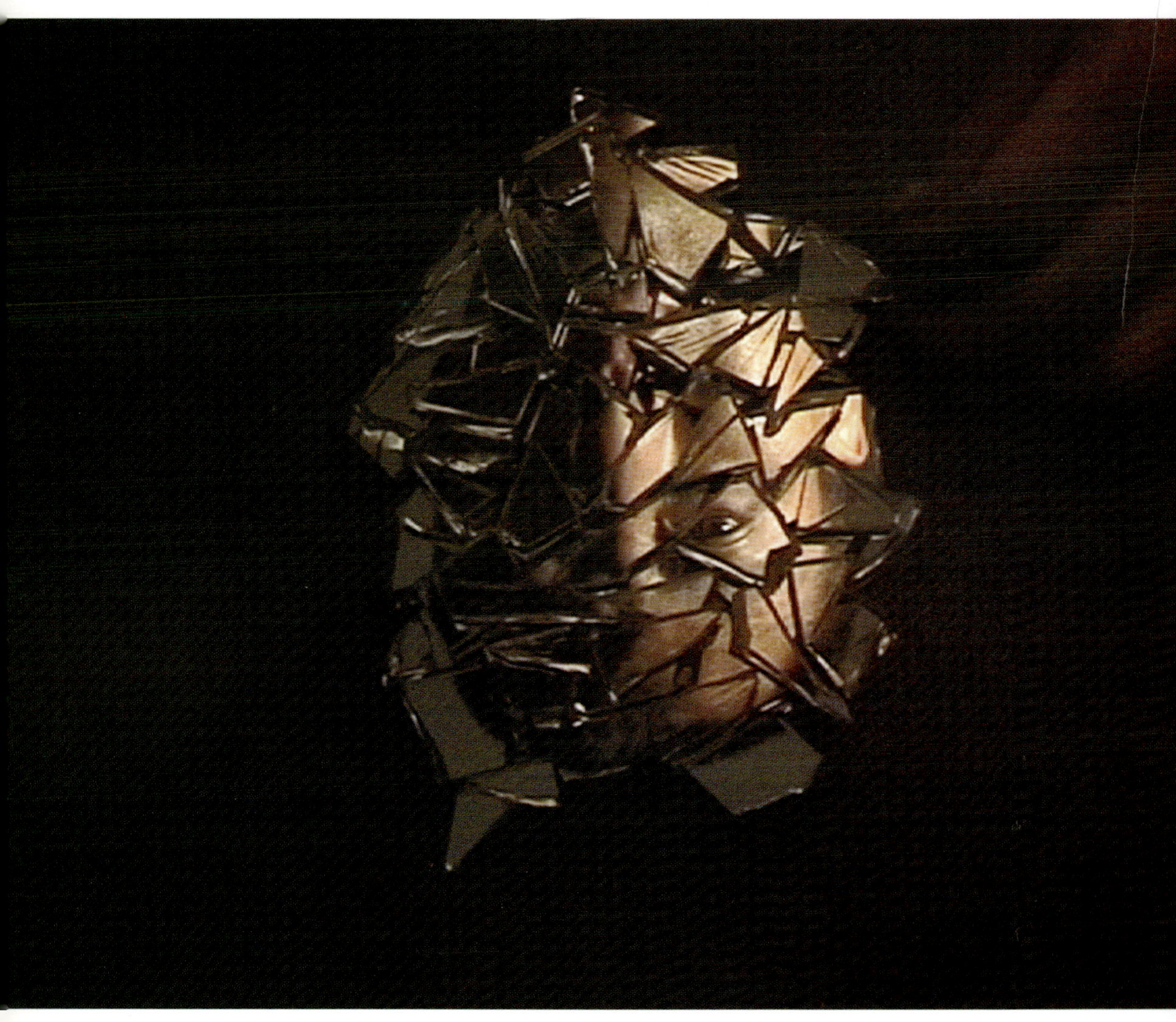

Face-VIII

Li Yongbin, 2000

video, single channel, 60 minutes, video still

The images show the artist piecing together a broken mirror in which his face is being reflected.

脸——8

李永斌，1998

单视频录像，六十分钟

该录像纪录这个艺术家正在拼凑着破碎的镜子，他的面孔照映在镜子
上，在这一行为过程中，艺术家的脸和镜子一起逐渐的完整起来。

40

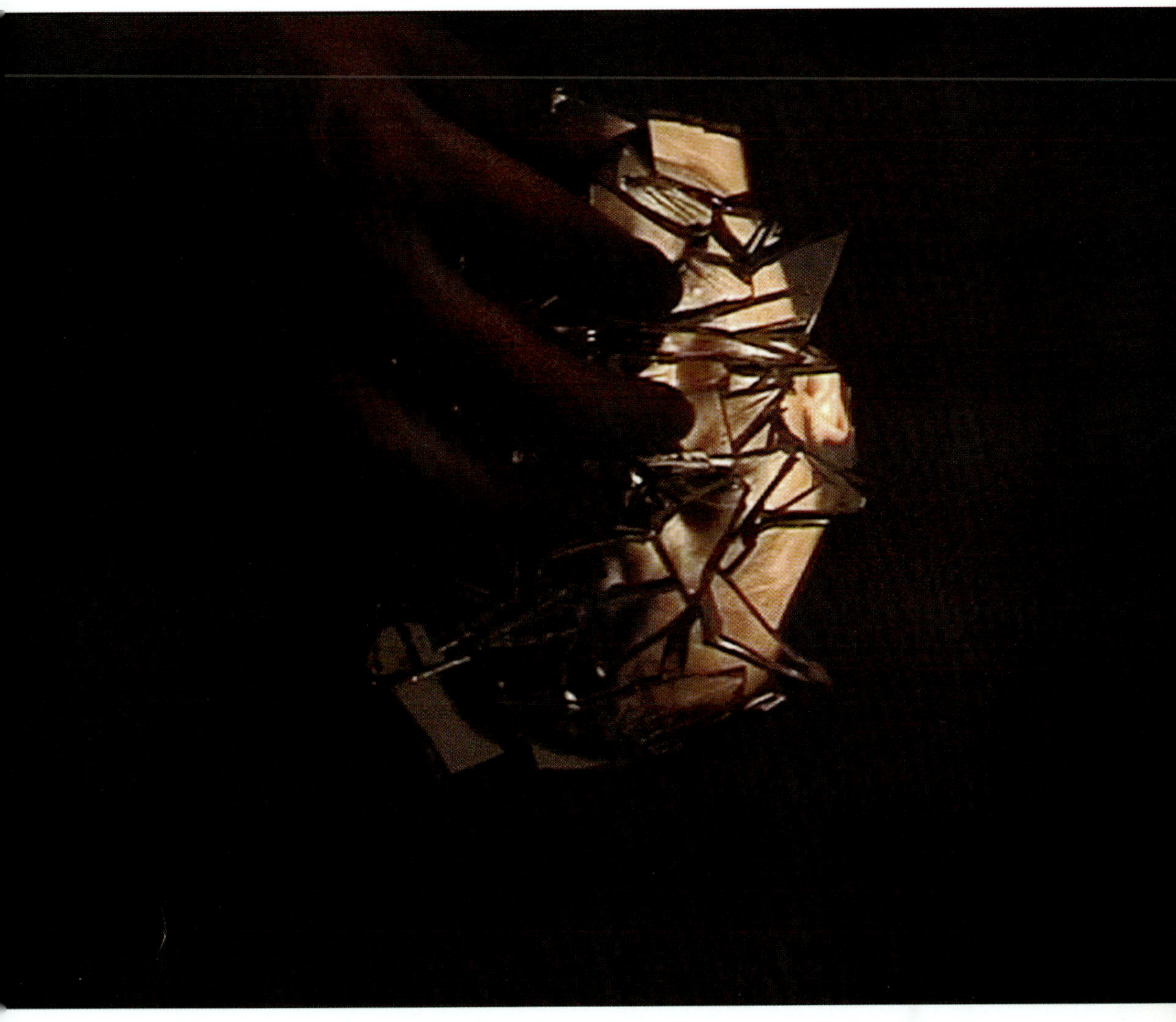

Ni Haifeng

Unfinished Self-Portrait II
Ni Haifeng, 2004
installation, acrylic paint, writings on glass

未完成自拍像 - 第二部分
倪海峰，2004
装置，丙稀颜料，玻璃上书写

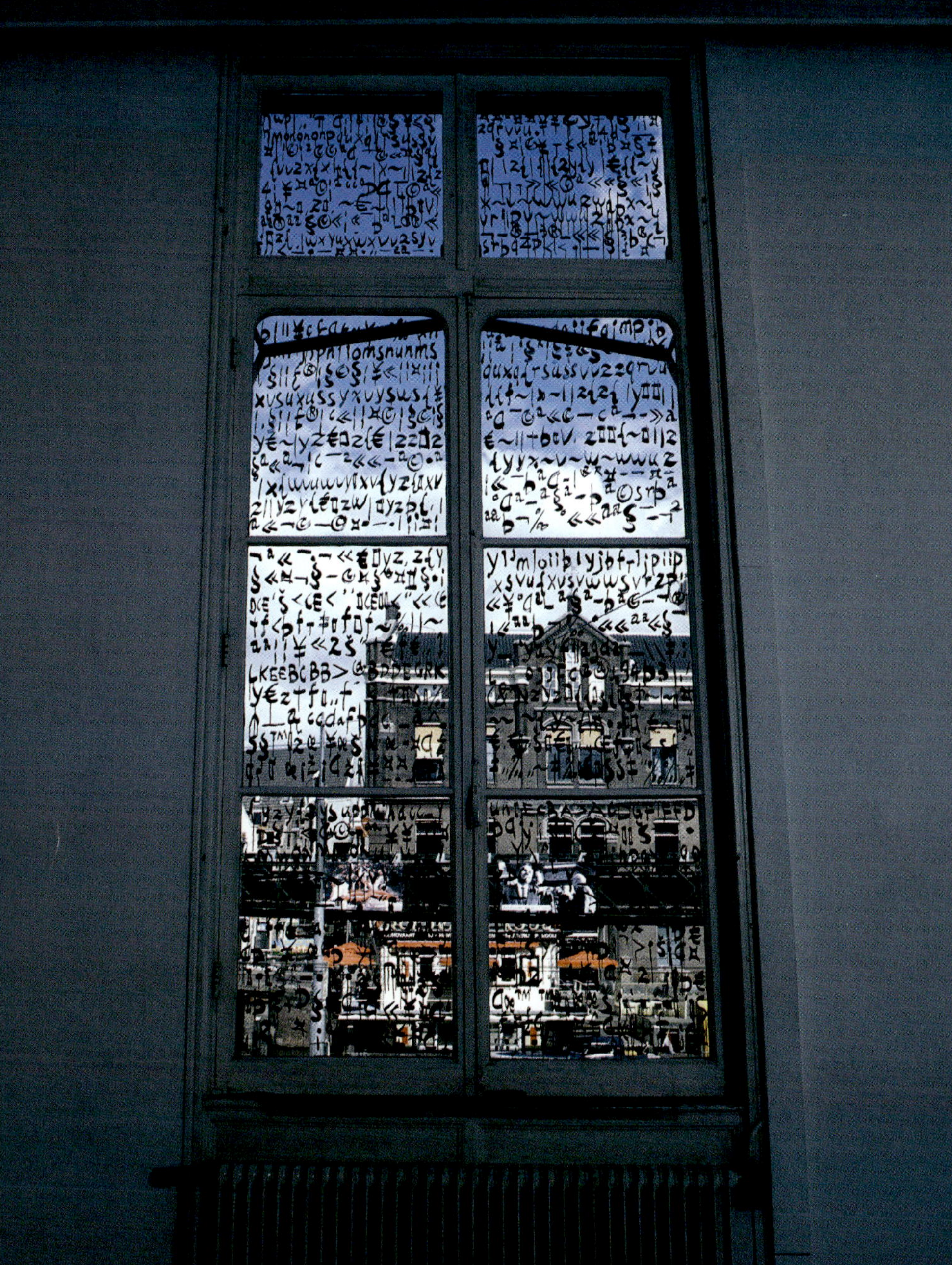

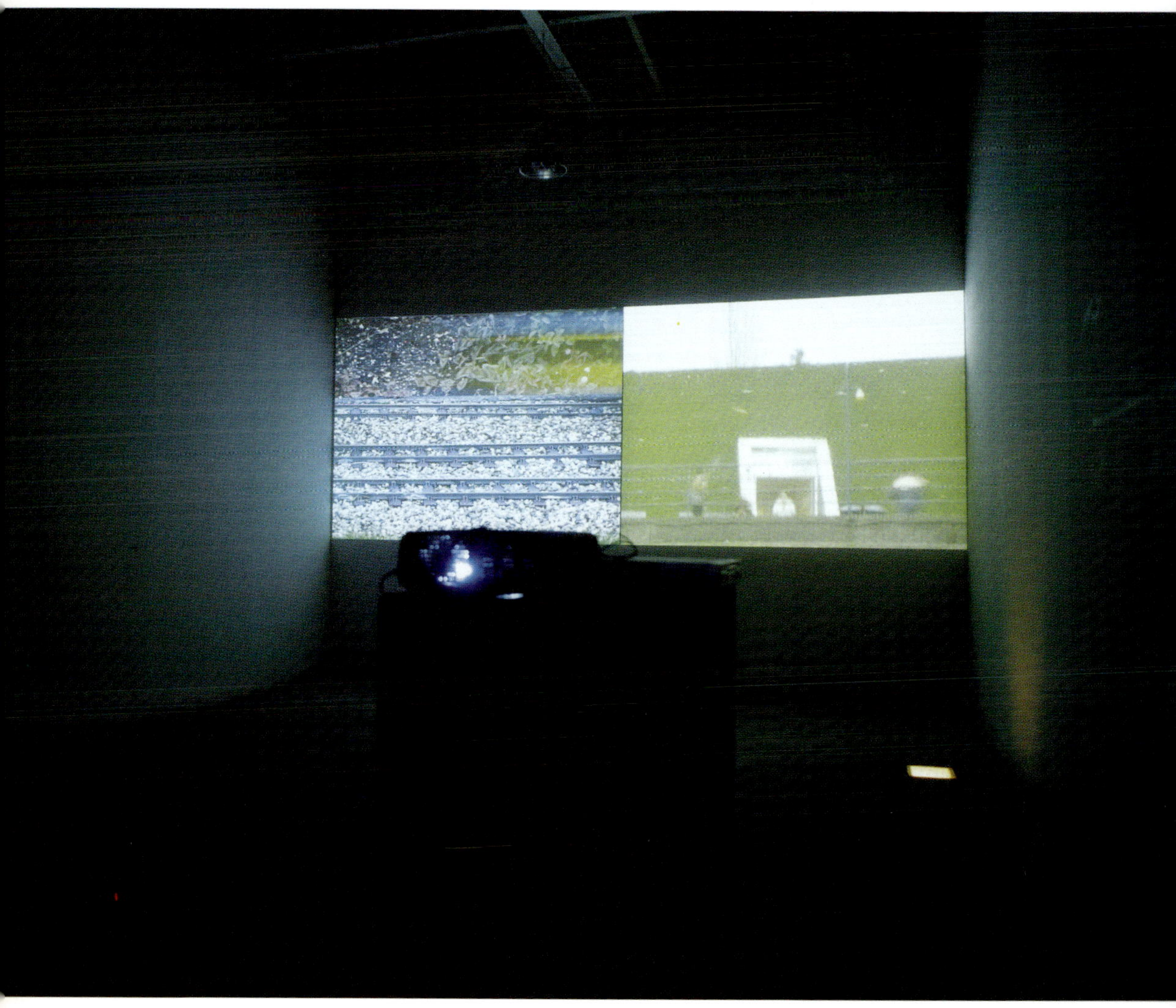

Multiple Lies

Ni Haifeng, 2002

video installation, 4 channels, 1 soundtrack, 2 video projections, 2 monitors, dimensions variable

Installation at EMAC, Beijing (China), 2002

The installation shows scenes from the famous Dutch miniature city Madurodam. Images of a foreign family visiting the theme park threaten to dissolve the Dutchness of the scenery, while canned sounds from the Dutch national anthem are being blared

多重谎言

倪海峰，2002

4 视频录像装置，单声道，2 部投影机，2 台监视器，可变尺寸，

远洋艺术中心，北京，中国，2002

这一关于荷兰的缩微城 Madurodam 的录像装置由两个并置的投影与两个监视器构成。其中一个投影展示一个正像化了的倒影，伴随着现场环境声：各种杂音与一曲听似廉价的荷兰国歌。其它三个通道录像分别记录这一"微缩现实"中的各种都市风景：机场、铁路、高速公路等。

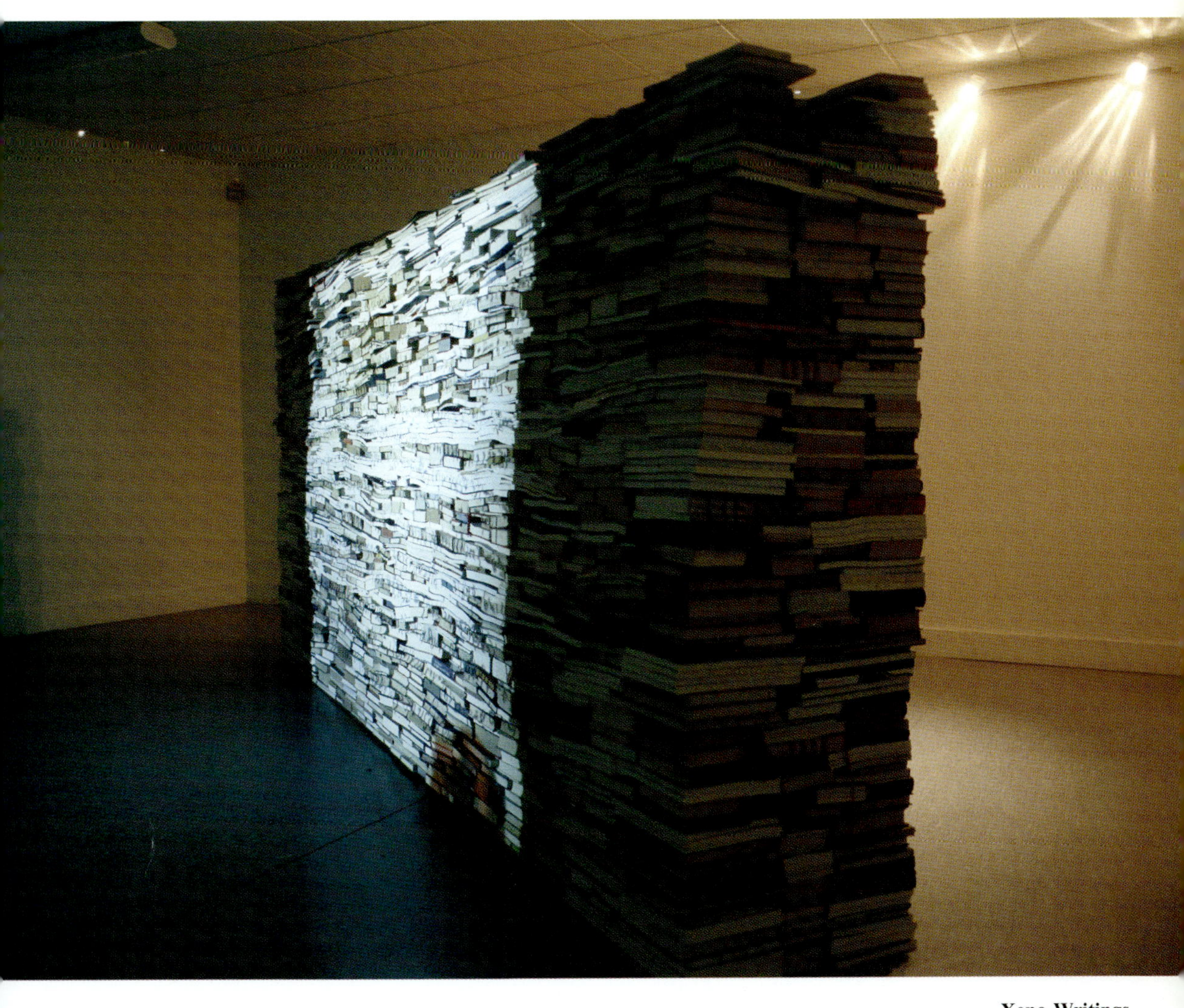

Xeno-Writings
Ni Haifeng, 2003
installation, books, video projection, dimensions variable,
installation at Museum Het Domein, Sittard (The Netherlands), 2004

外来的写作
倪海峰，2003
装置，书，录像投影，可变尺寸，Het Domein 博物馆，荷兰，2004

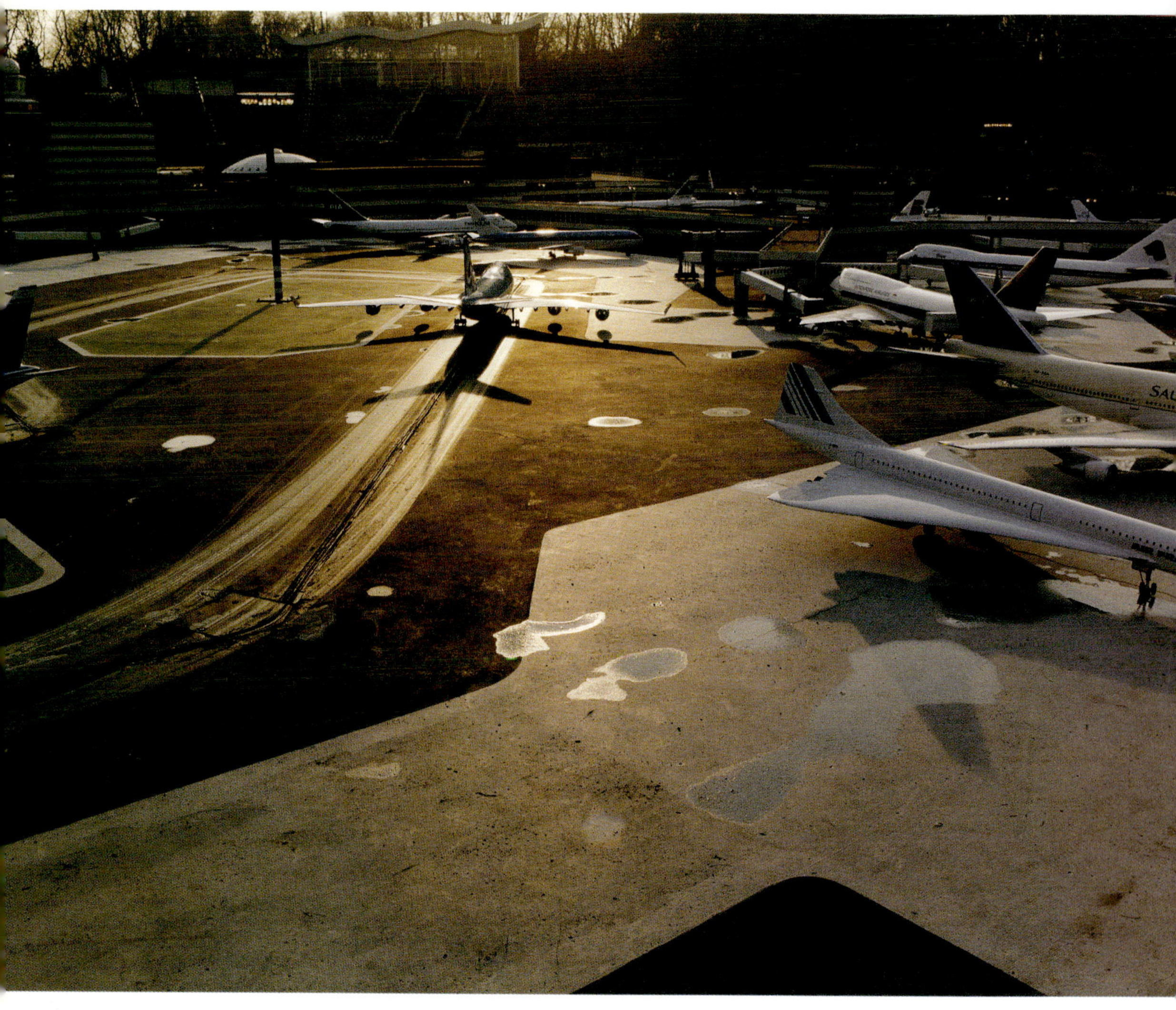

No - Man's - Land

Ni Haifeng, 1999 - 2001

photographic series, total 14, 127cm x 100cm

无人之城

倪海峰，1999 — 2001

照片，总共 14 张，127x100 厘米

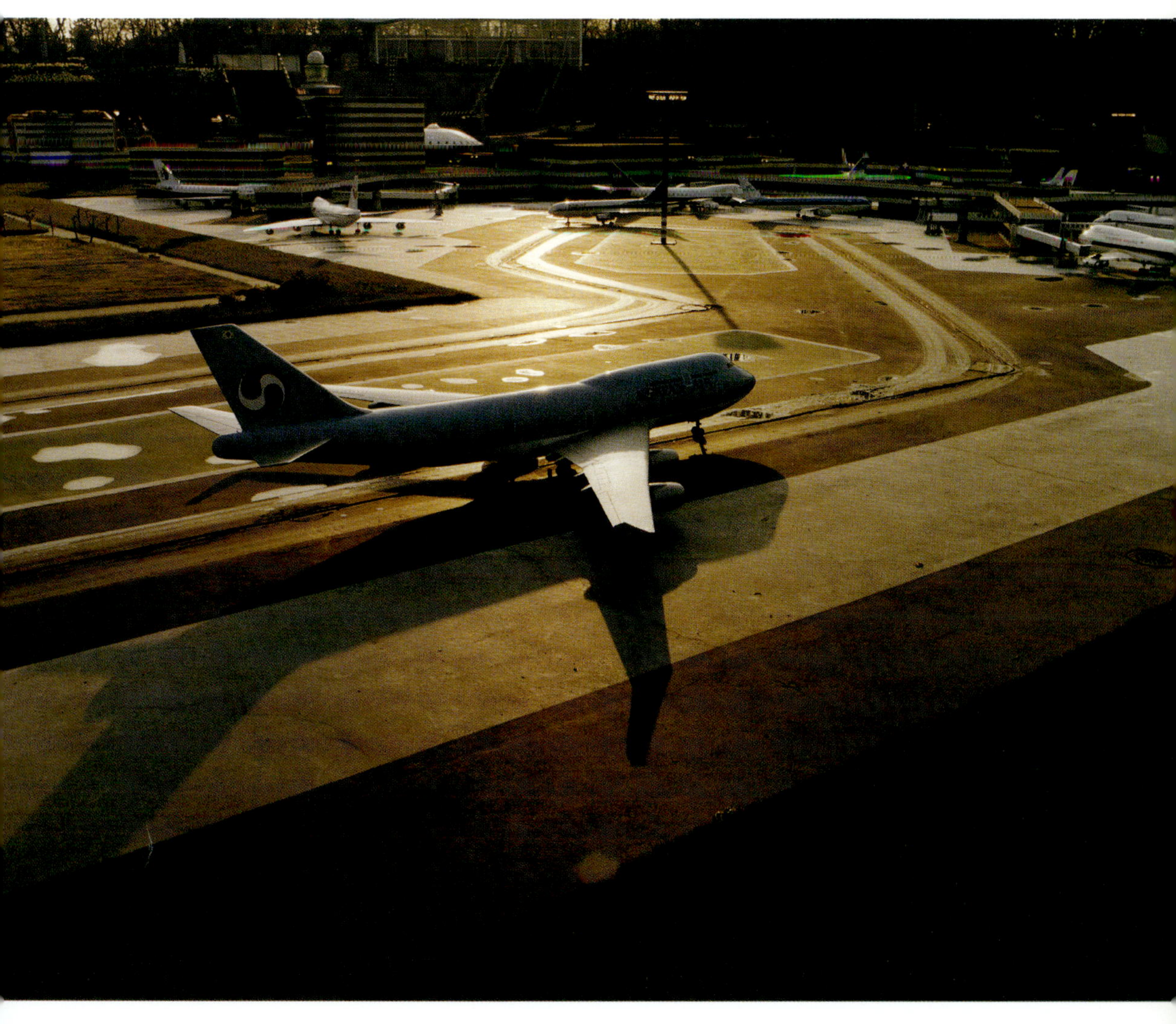

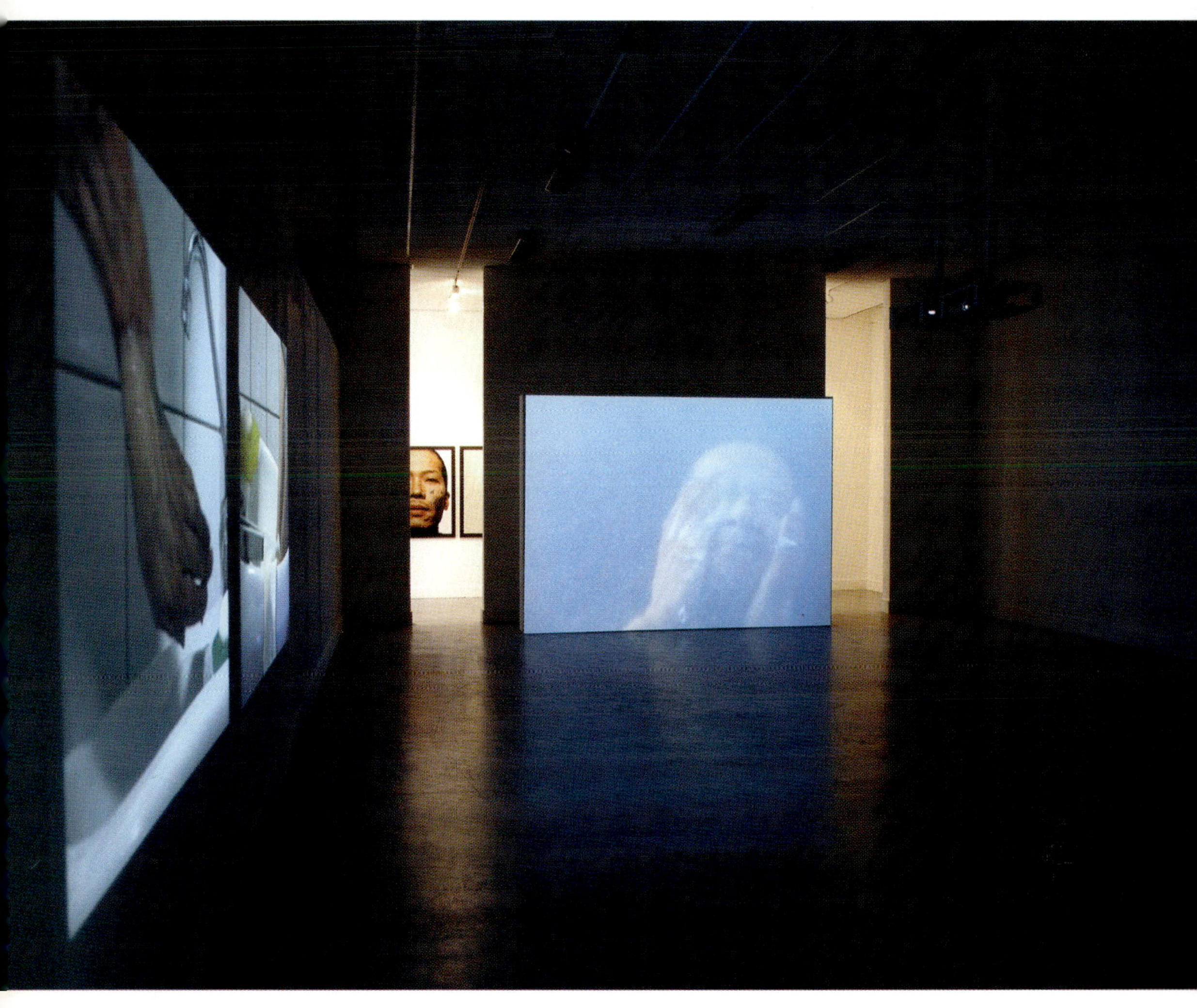

Installation View:
(left) **Washing Hands** (2003)
(right) **The Face** (2004)

展览场景：（左）洗手(2003)，（右）脸(2004)

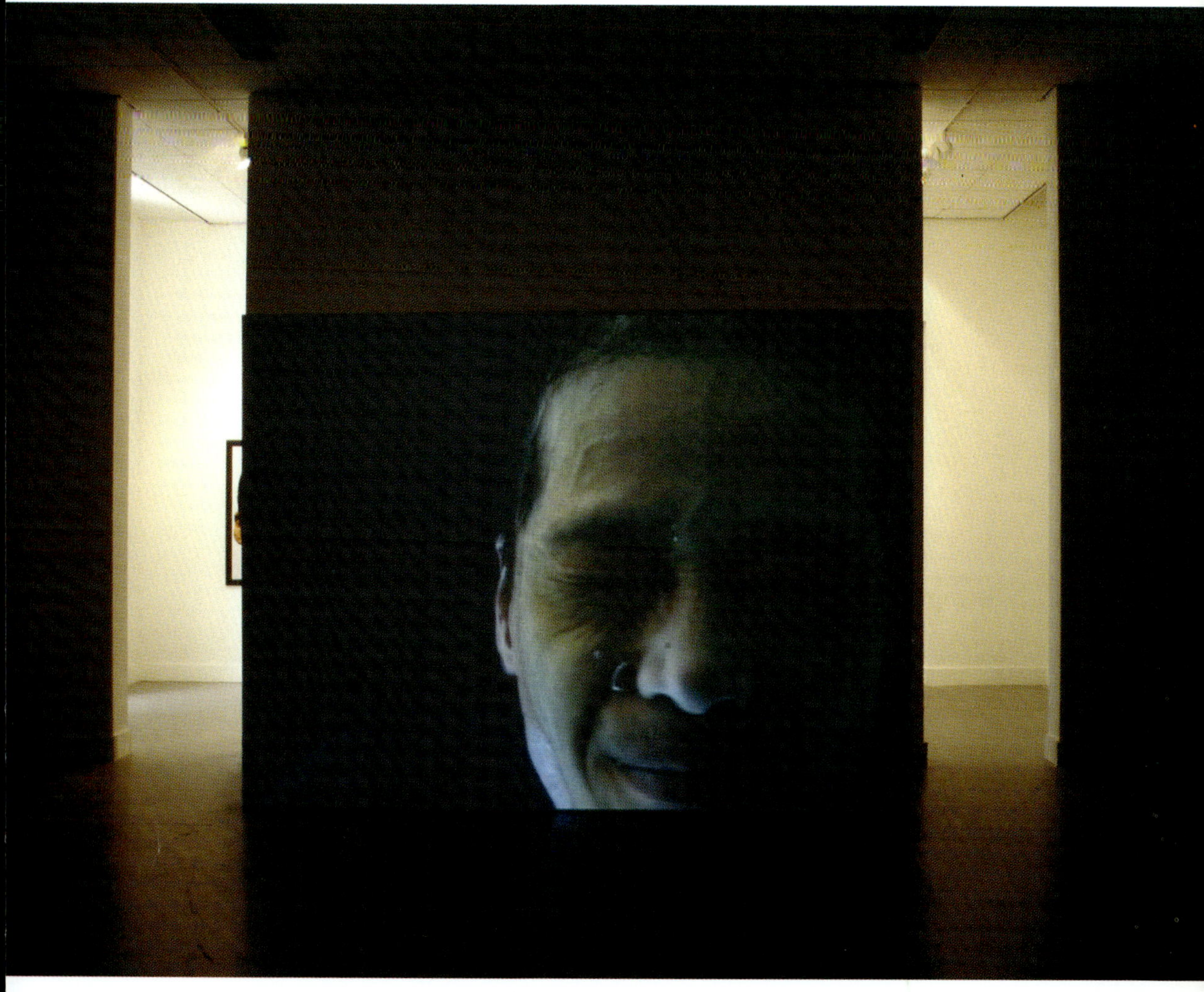

The Face
Ni Haifeng, 2004
video installation, single channel, dimensions variable, 14 minutes
installation at Museum Het Domein, Sittard (The Netherlands)

The images, recorded from an under-water angle, show a person repeatedly washing his face. The face is gradually eclipsed by the
soapy water. Silent at the beginning, the washing process is gradually engulfed in the great noise of the city outside.

脸
倪海峰，2004
录像装置，可变尺寸，Het Domein 博物馆，荷兰 2004
这个影像是在水中从水底往上拍一个人重复洗脸的过程。在清洗过程中，水由清澈变混浊直至洗脸者的形象从浊水中消失。录像的
前半部分无声，当洗脸者的形象开始消失的时候，各种城市噪音逐渐进入画面。作品以强噪音收尾。

Shi Yong

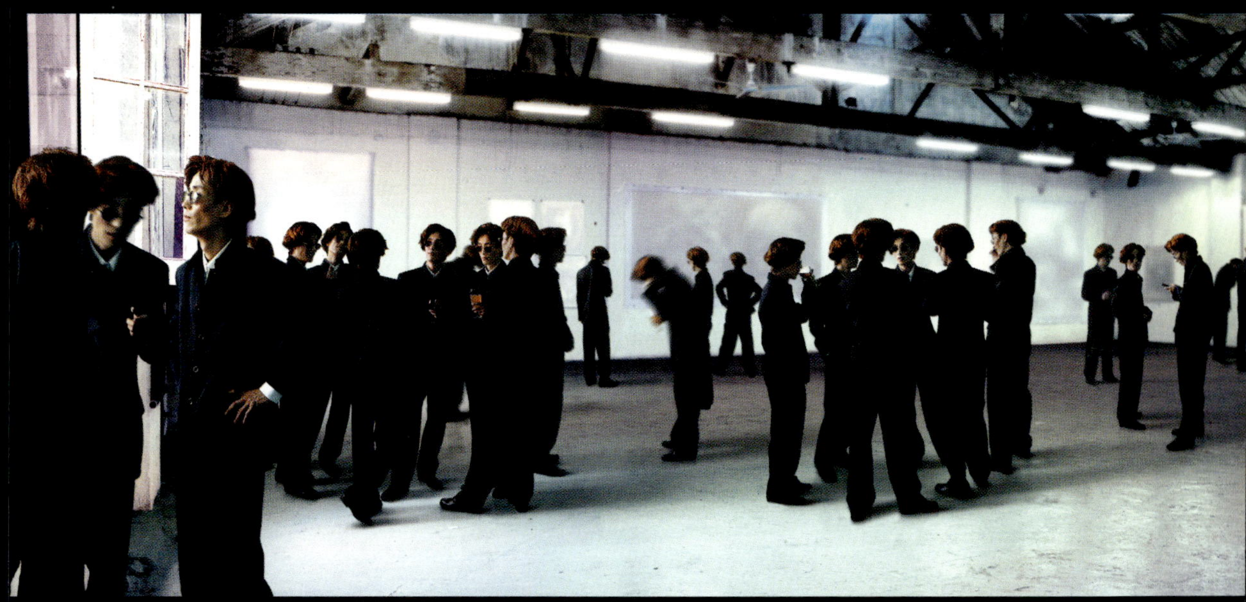

The Moon Tonight - Gallery Scenery No.1
Shi Yong, 2002
digital photograph, 360cm x 80cm

施勇

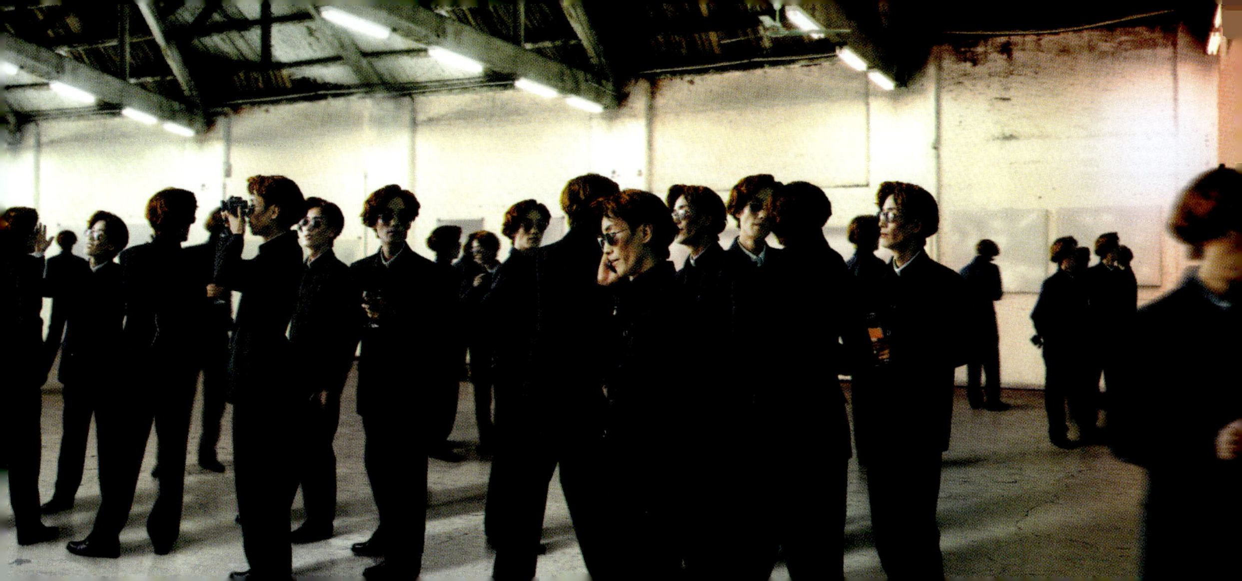

QQ's Illusion

Shi Yong, 2002

video projection, soundtrack, loudspeakers, polythene screen,

installation at EMAC, Beijing (China), 2002

The projection on a polythene film screen shows the image of a person gesturing wildly. Eight loudspeakers have been placed at the corners of the screen. The man's gestures generate violent sounds and the screen moves accordingly.

QQ 的幻想

施勇，2002

装置，投影，声音，塑料薄膜，8 只扬声器，远洋艺术中心，北京，中国，2002

一个打着各种手势的男人形象被投射在一张塑料薄膜上，裸露的扬声器放置在塑料薄膜的各个角落。这些手势产生猛烈的声音，屏幕因此震动起来。

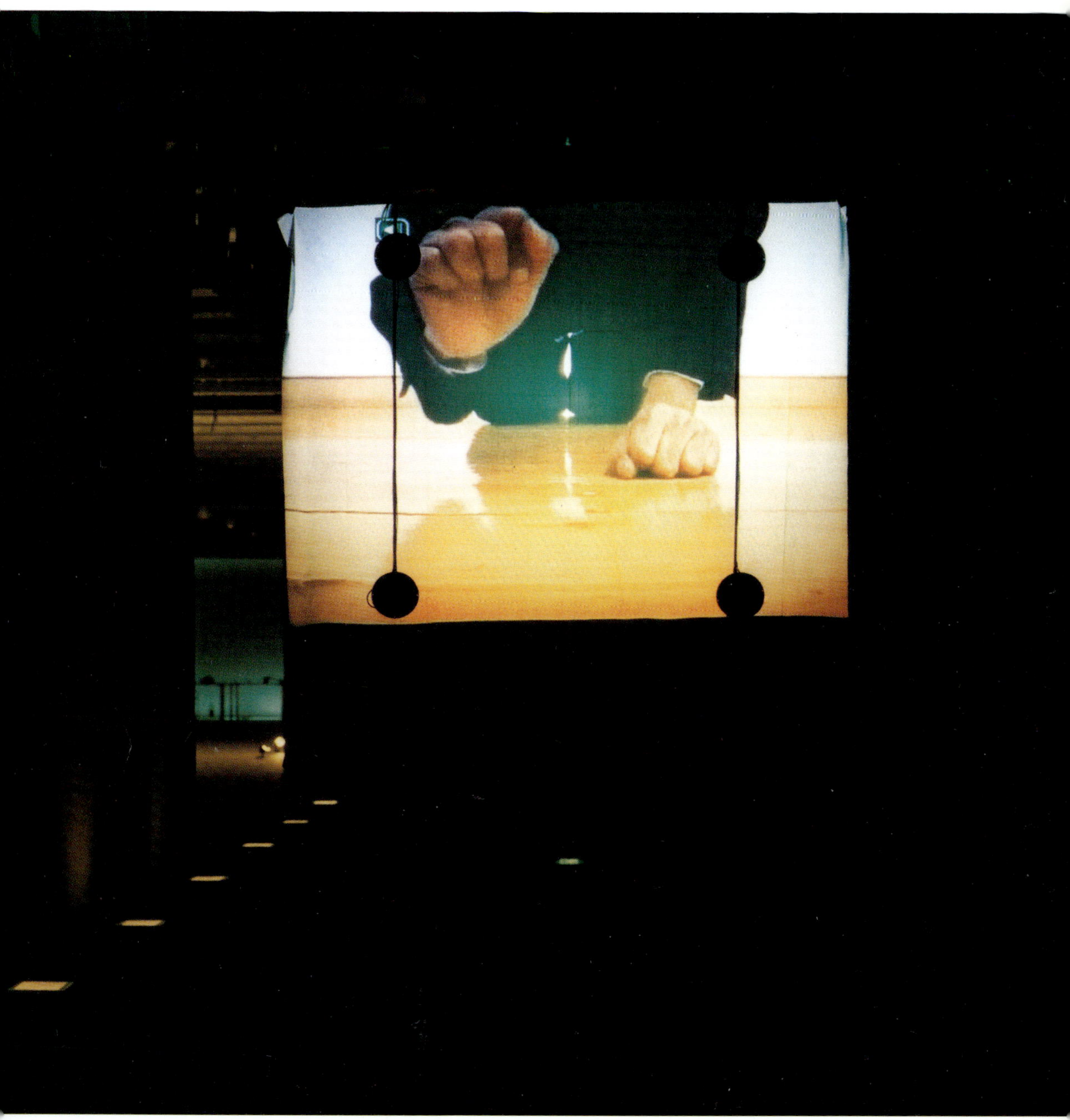

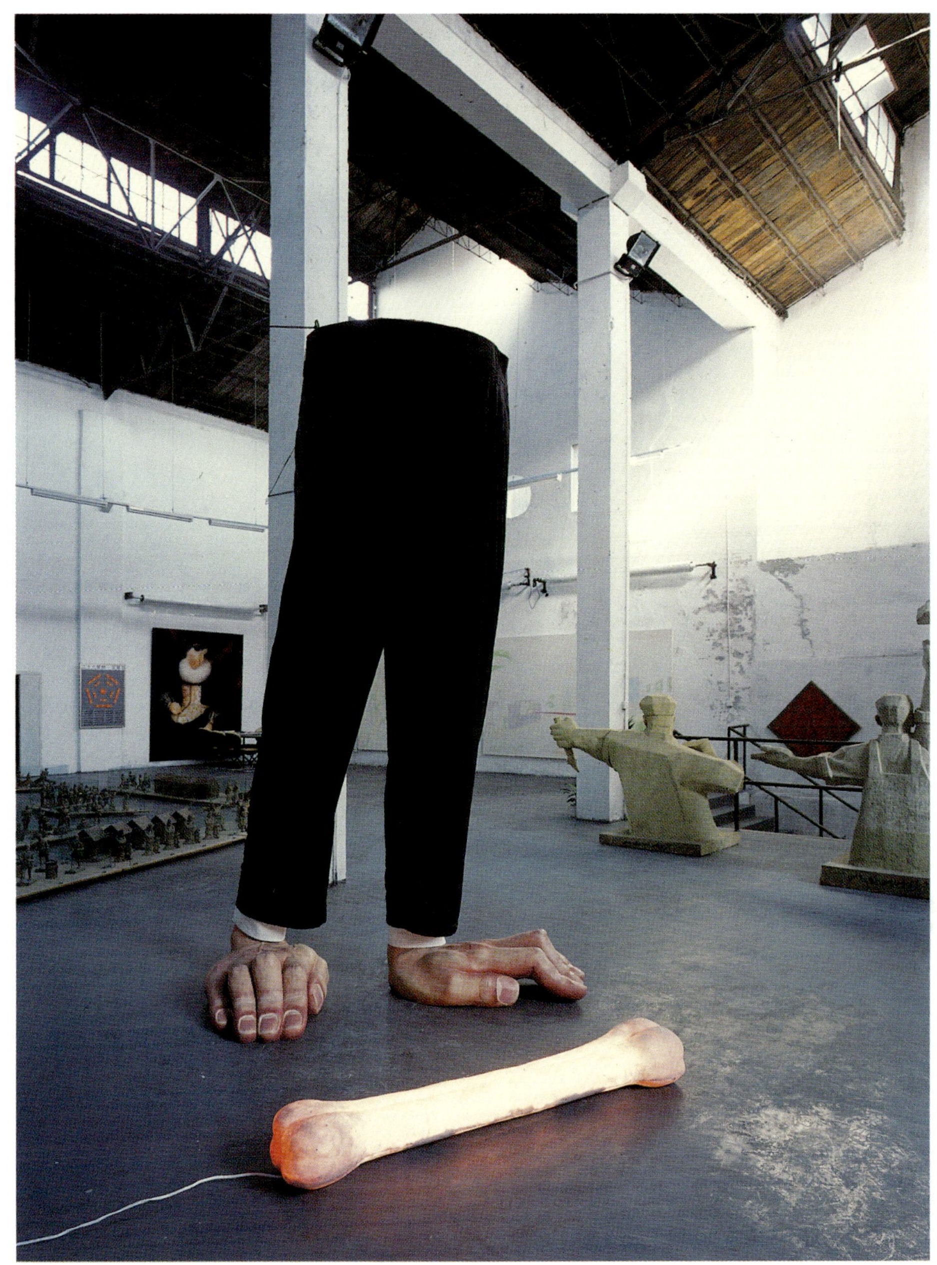

The Tantalizing Moonlight

Shi Yong, 2002

installation, colored fiberglass, cloth, sound, ca. 300cm x 165cm x 170cm

月色撩人

施勇，2002

着色玻璃钢，布，音响，300x165x170(厘米)

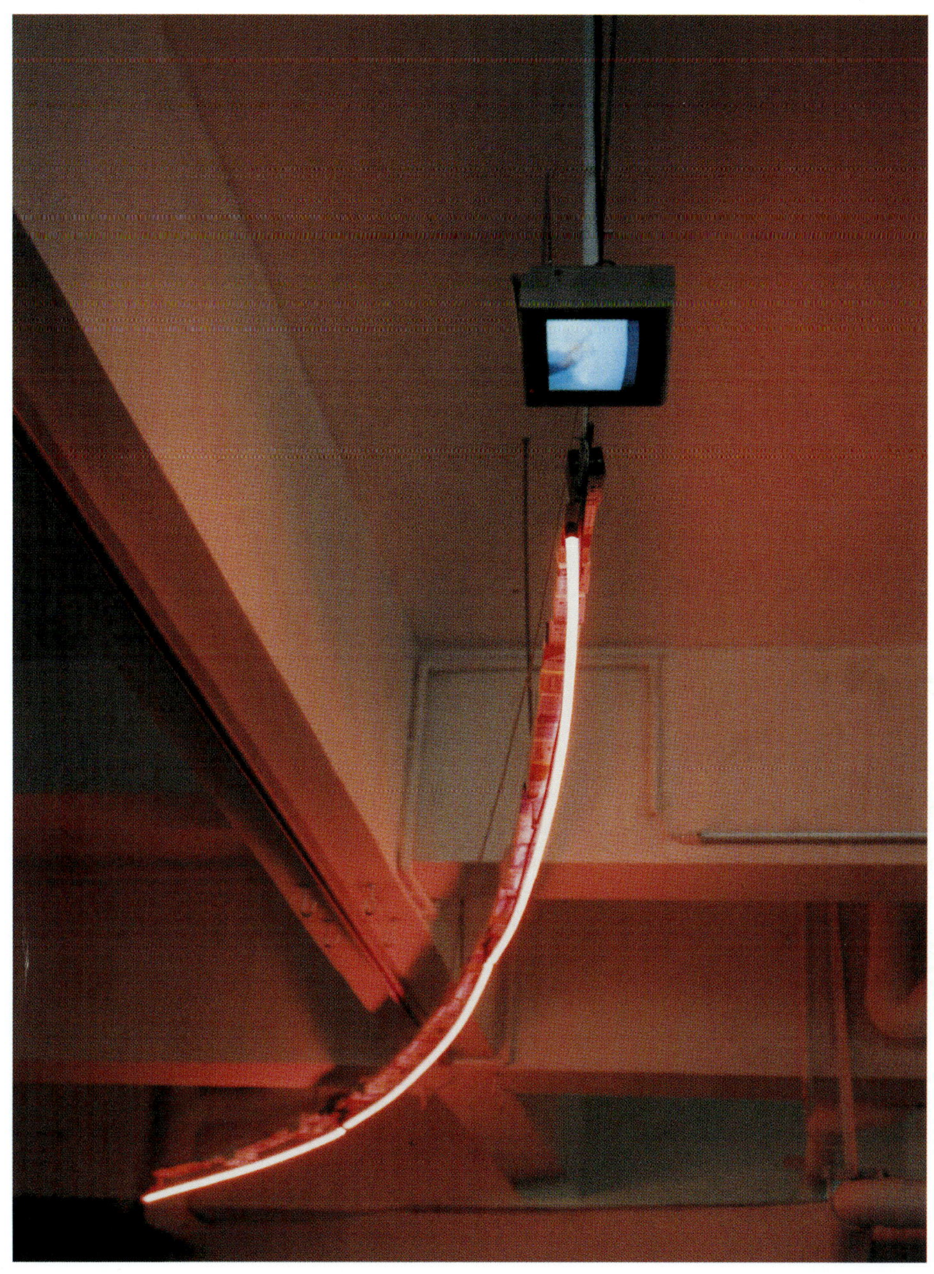

Flying Higher and Higher
Shi Yong, 2002
video installation

可以飞的更高
施勇，2002
录像装置

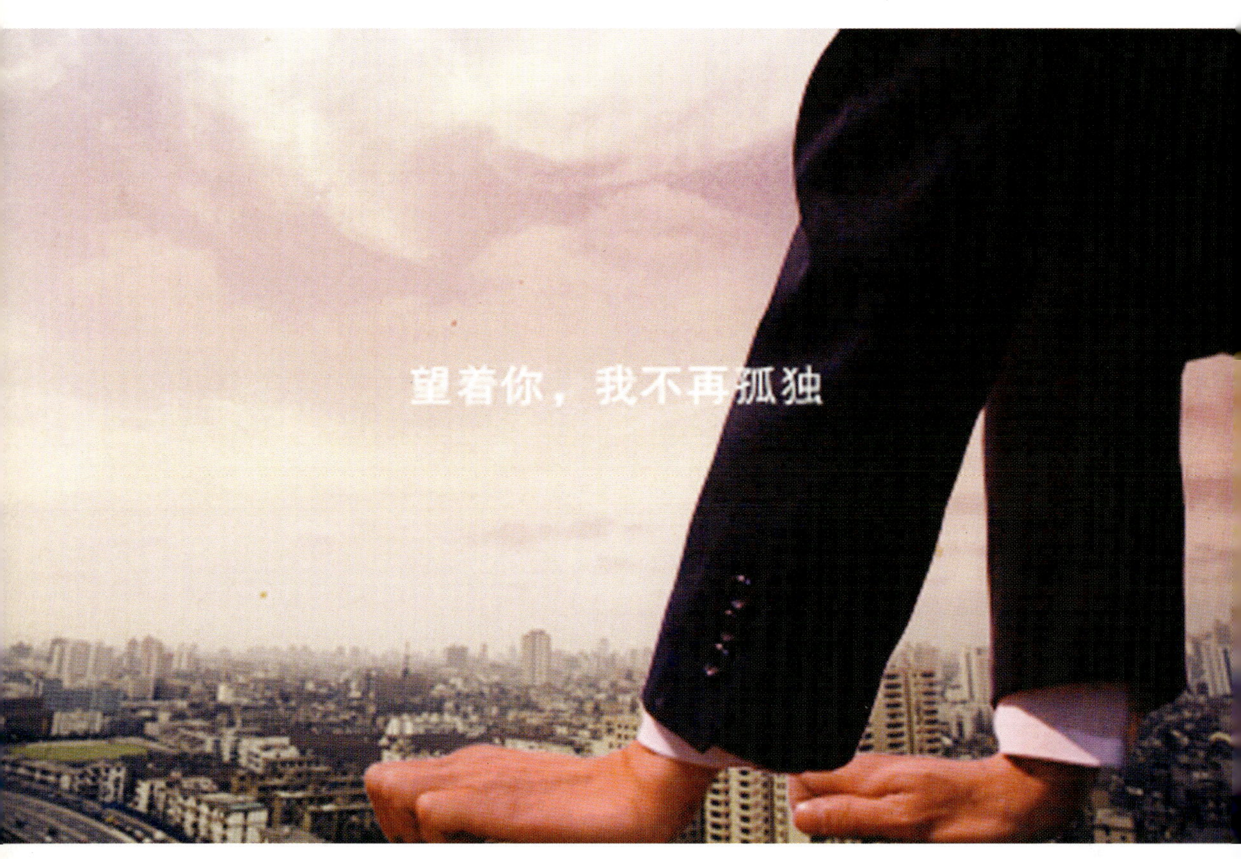

The Universe of Desire
Shi Yong, 2002
installation, ca. 600cm x 400cm x 240cm
video still

欲望星空
施勇 2002
装置，600 × 400 × 240（厘米）
录像照片

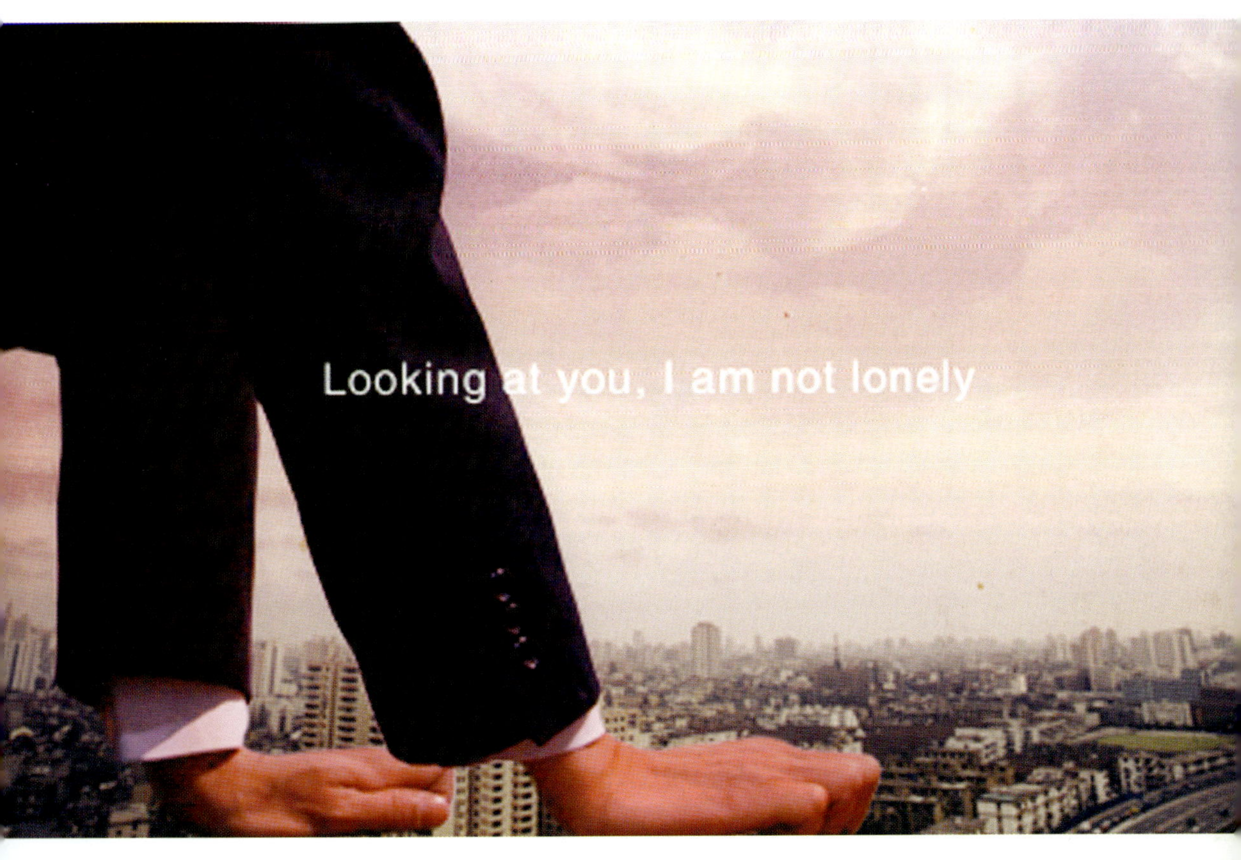

Looking at you, I am not lonely

Wang Gongxin

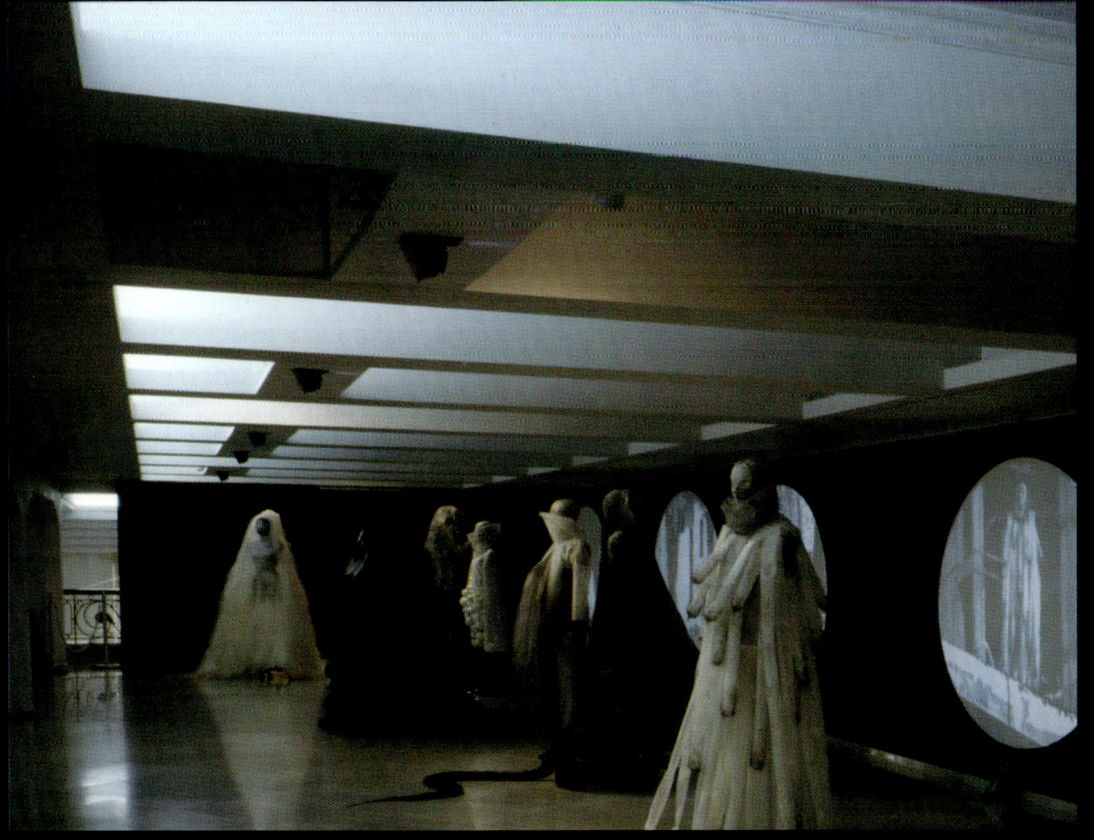

Here or There

Wang Gongxin and Lin Tianmiao, 2002

6 video projections, 9 objects, dimensions variable, installation at Shanghai Art Museum,

Shanghai (China), 2002

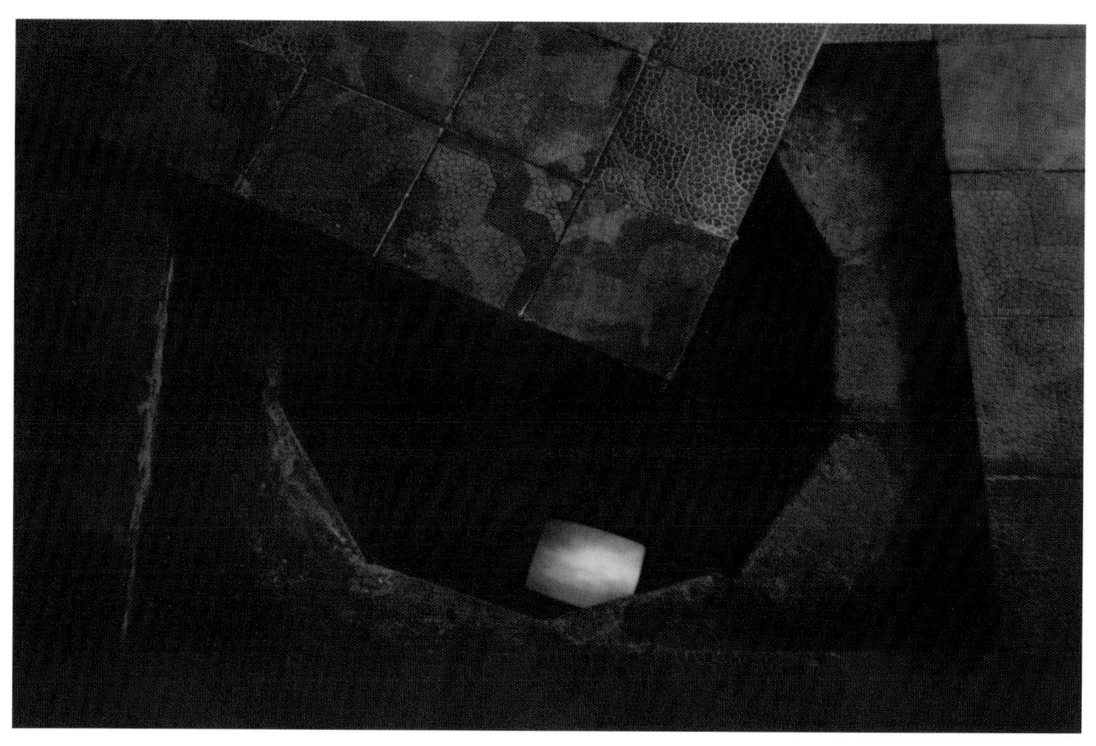

The Sky of Brooklyn
Wang Gongxin, 1995
installation, monitor, video, soundtrack, loop
The artist dug a hole in the living room of his home in Beijing.
At the bottom of the hole, a monitor shows the sky of Brooklyn.

布鲁克林的天空
王功新，1995
录像装置，监视器，声音，循环播放
艺术家在北京家里的卧室中挖了一个洞，洞底有一监视器显示着
布鲁克林的天空。

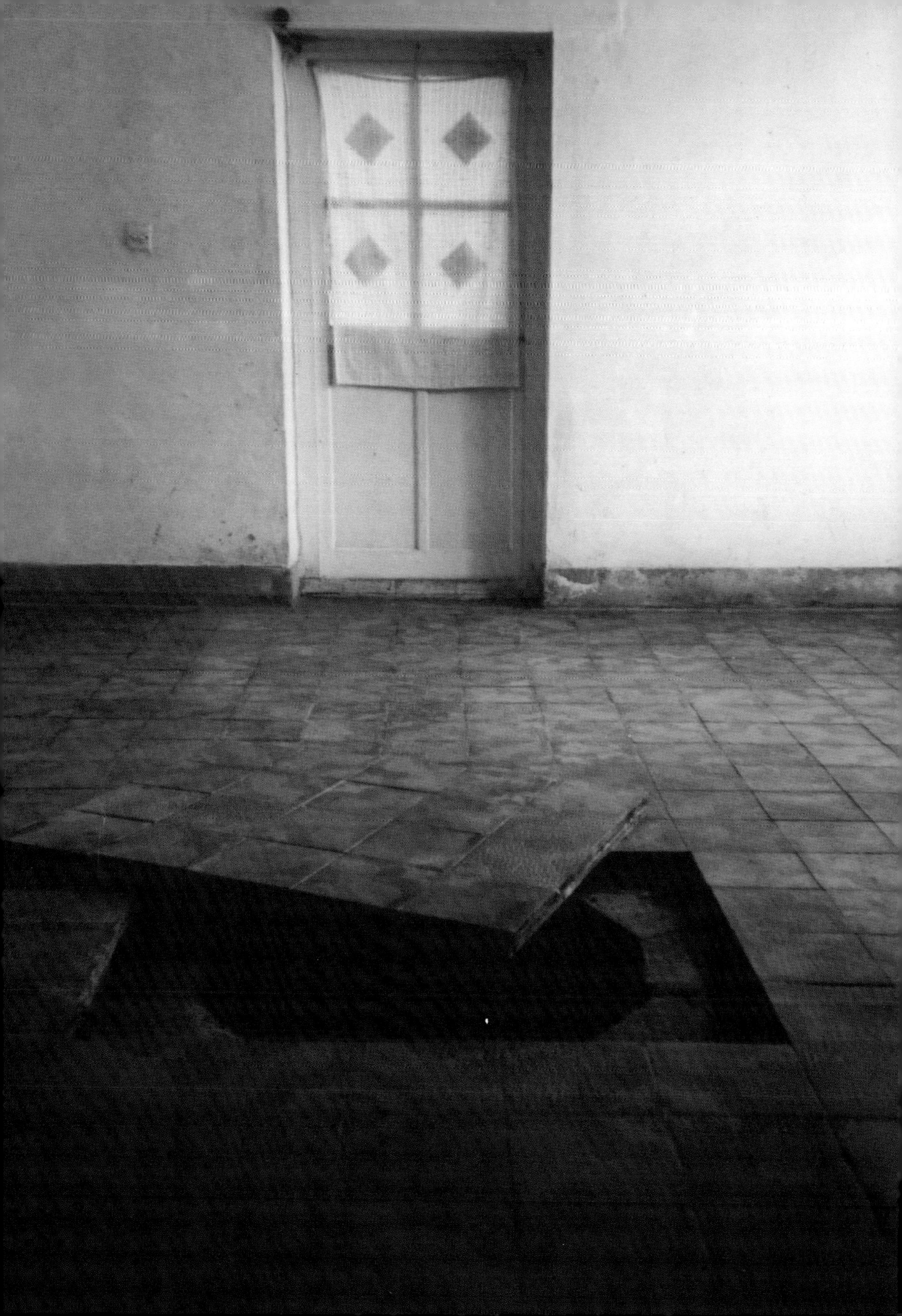

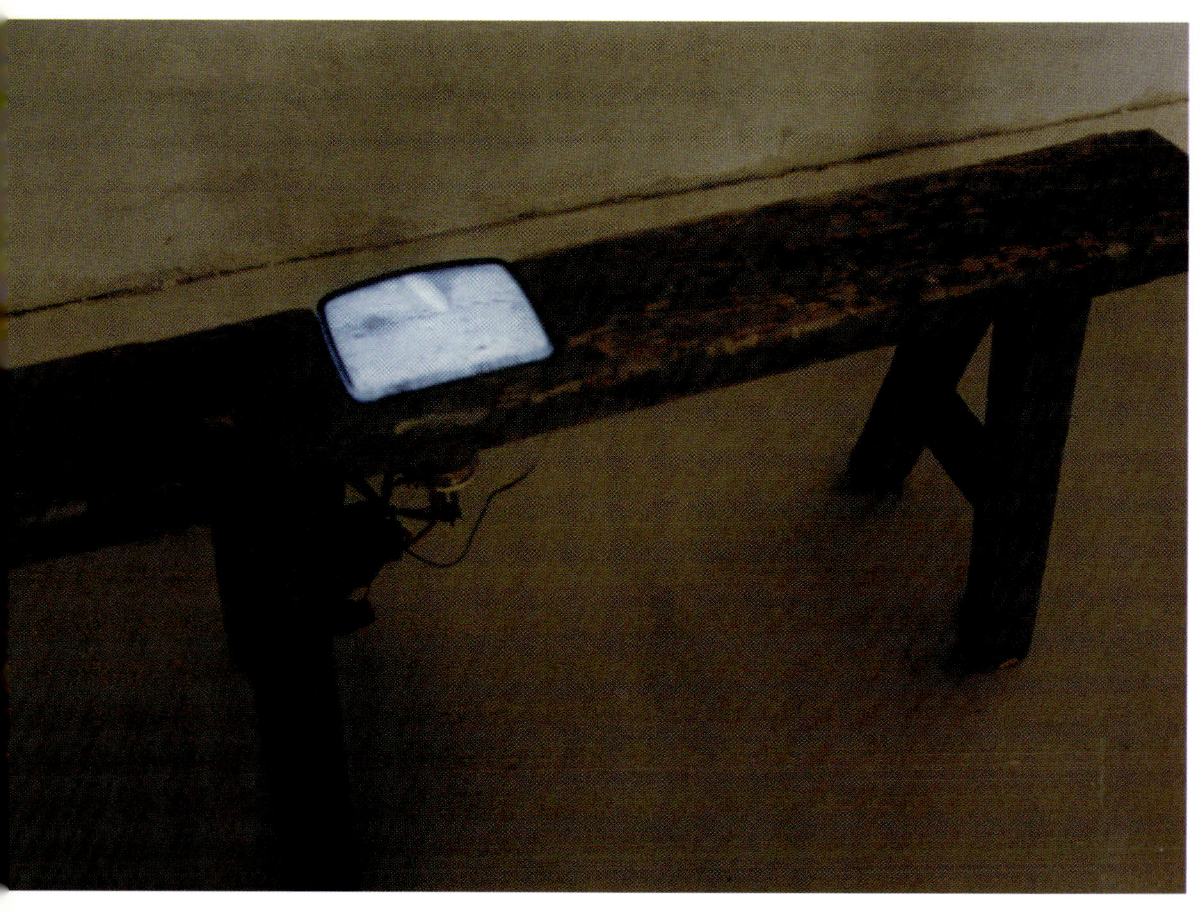

Old Bench

Wang Gongxin, 1997

video installation, wooden bench, monitor

The image on the bench shows a finger touching the part of the bench that is replaced by the monitor.

老凳子

王功新，1997

录像装置，木凳，小型监视器

板凳上的影像是一个手指，正在触摸板凳上被监视器所取代的这一部分。

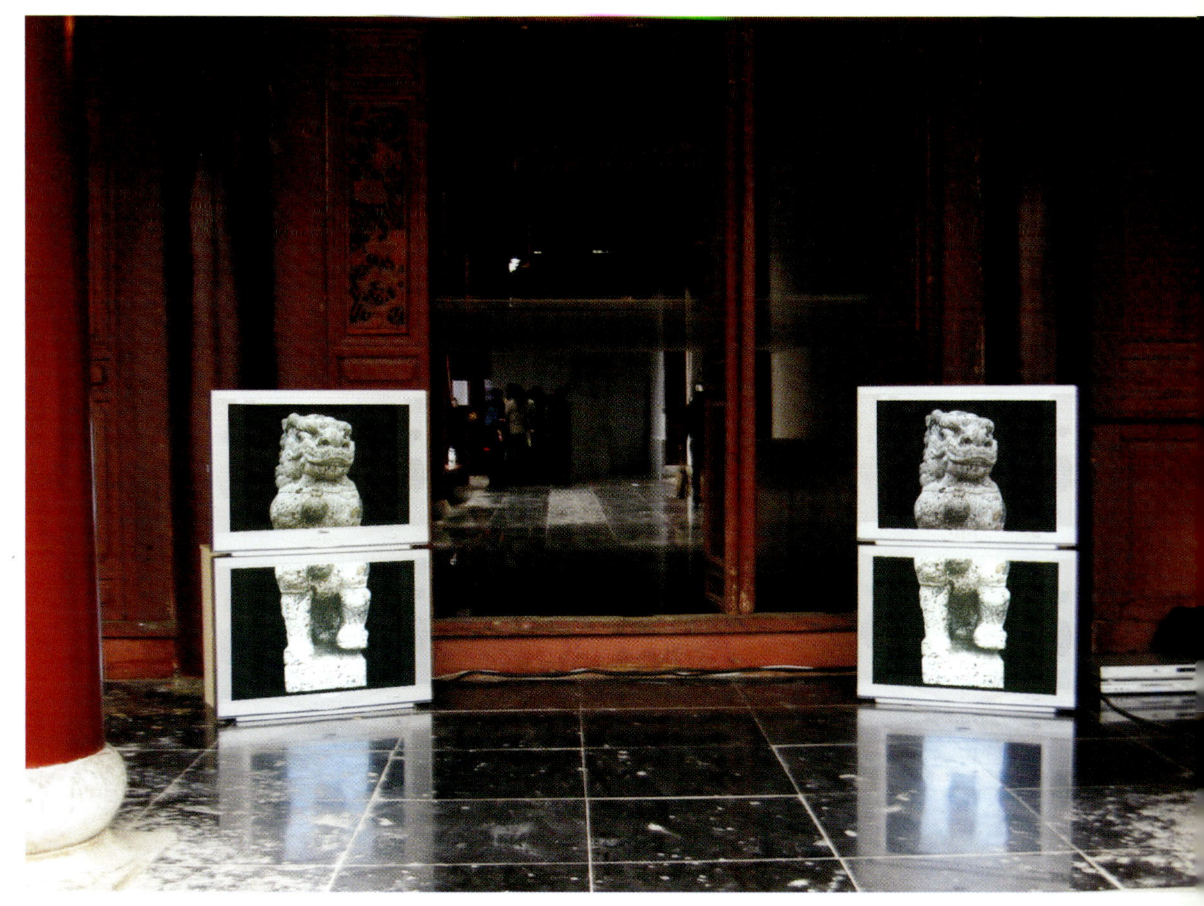

Always Welcome
Wang Gongxin, 2003
video installation

欧尾狮欢迎你
王功新，2003
录像装置

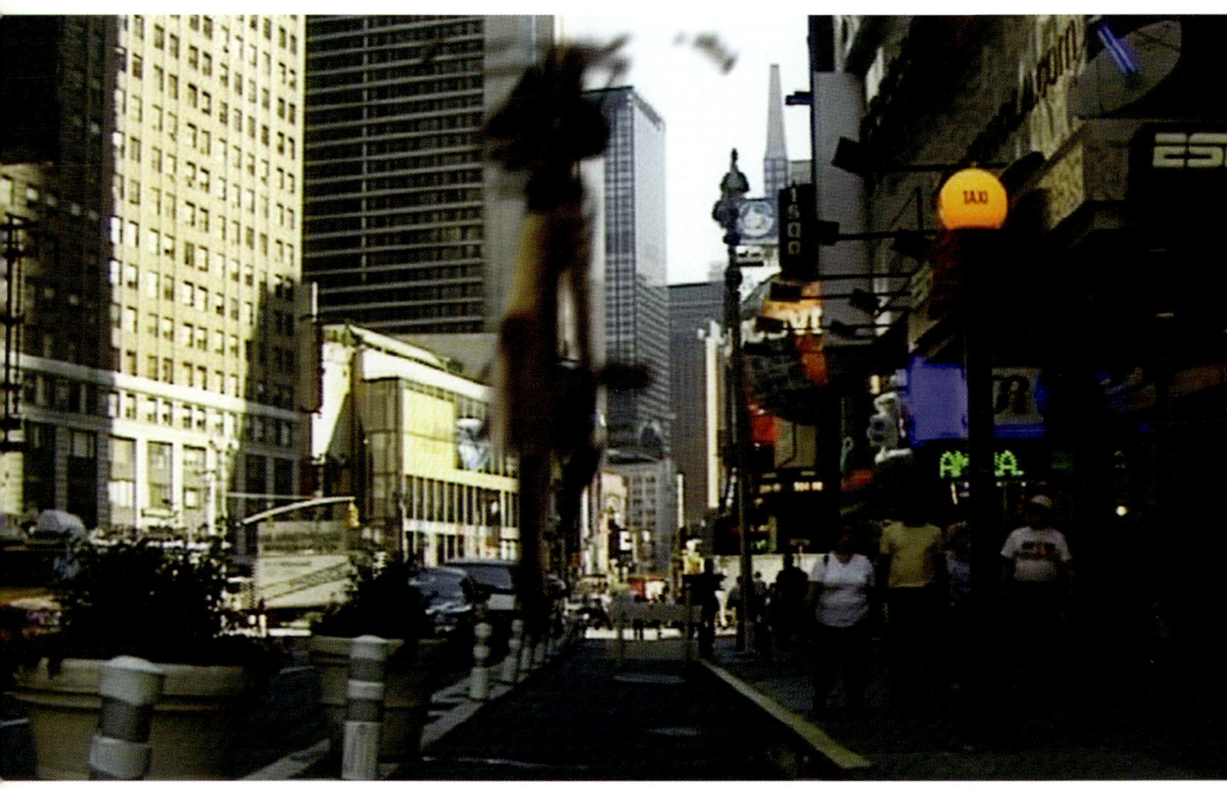

Go Beyond
Wang Gongxin, 2002
video projection, soundtrack, photograph on lightbox
installation at EMAC, Beijing (China), 2002
*The work consists of a video projection and a photograph on light box. The
photograph depicts the artist cycling through a suburb of Beijing. The video shows the
artist, falling naked through the air and landing in New York to be followed by a pile
of clothes and the bicycle.*

跨越
王功新，2002
录像装置，灯箱图片，声音，远洋艺术中心，北京，中国，2002
这个作品由一个录像投影和一个灯箱照片组成。照片展示的是艺术家本人骑车穿越北京
郊区。录像记录的是他赤身裸体坠落在纽约街头，他的一堆衣服和自行车也随之而落。

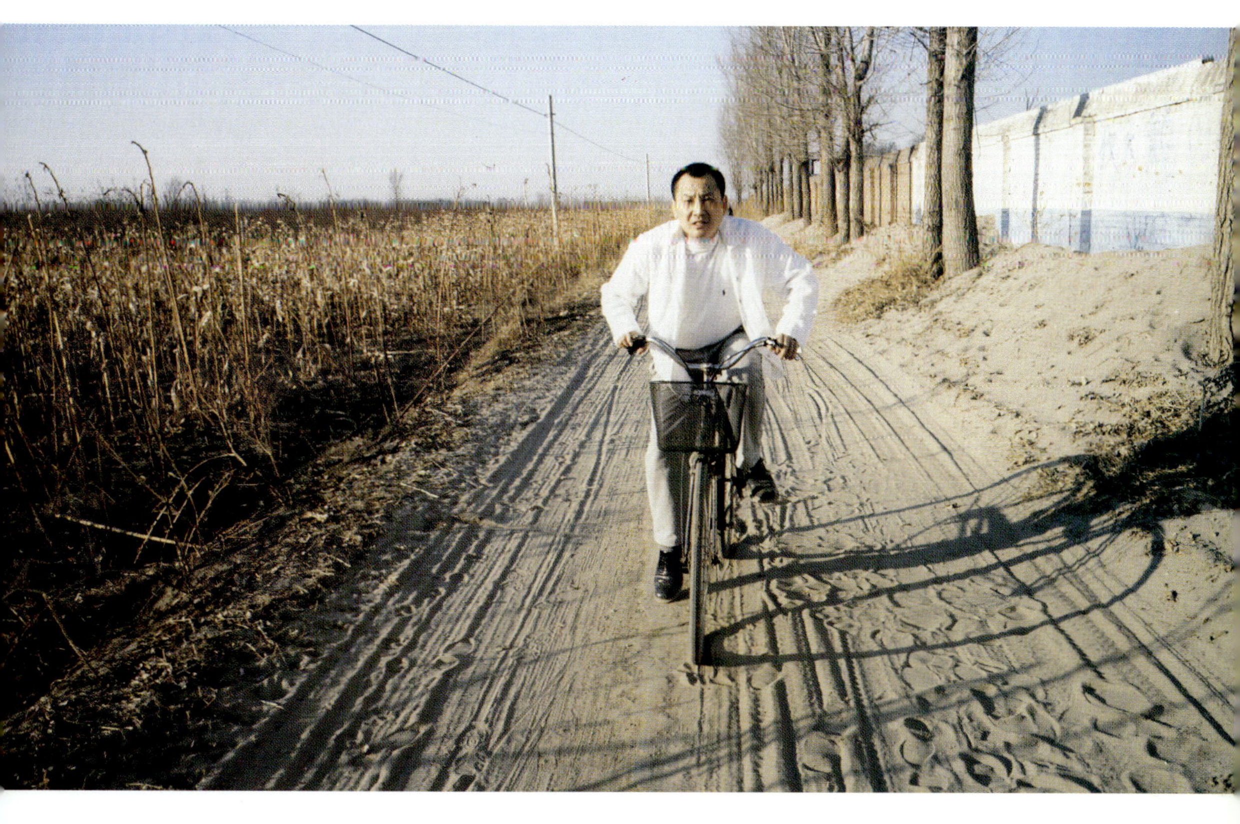

Wang Jianwei

My Visual Archive
Wang Jianwei, 2002
video installation, 2 channels, dimensions variable
iustallation at Museum of Asian CiviCizarion,singapre,2002
*The work investigates the visual representation of history and how cinema has become the
author of history. The installation consists of two video channels that are projected onto both
sides of a wall, one at the back of the other. One channel shows a compilation of fragments
from pre-Cultural Revolution movies, while the other shows fragments from the movies made
during the Cultural Revolution.*

我的视觉档案
汪建伟，2002
双通道录像装置，可变尺寸，新加坡亚洲文化博物馆 2002
这个装置是由两个视频构成的，它们分别被投射在一个屏幕的正反两面。一个视频展示的是文
革前各种电影中的＂视觉碎片＂的集合。另一个则是取自文革期间的各种电影。

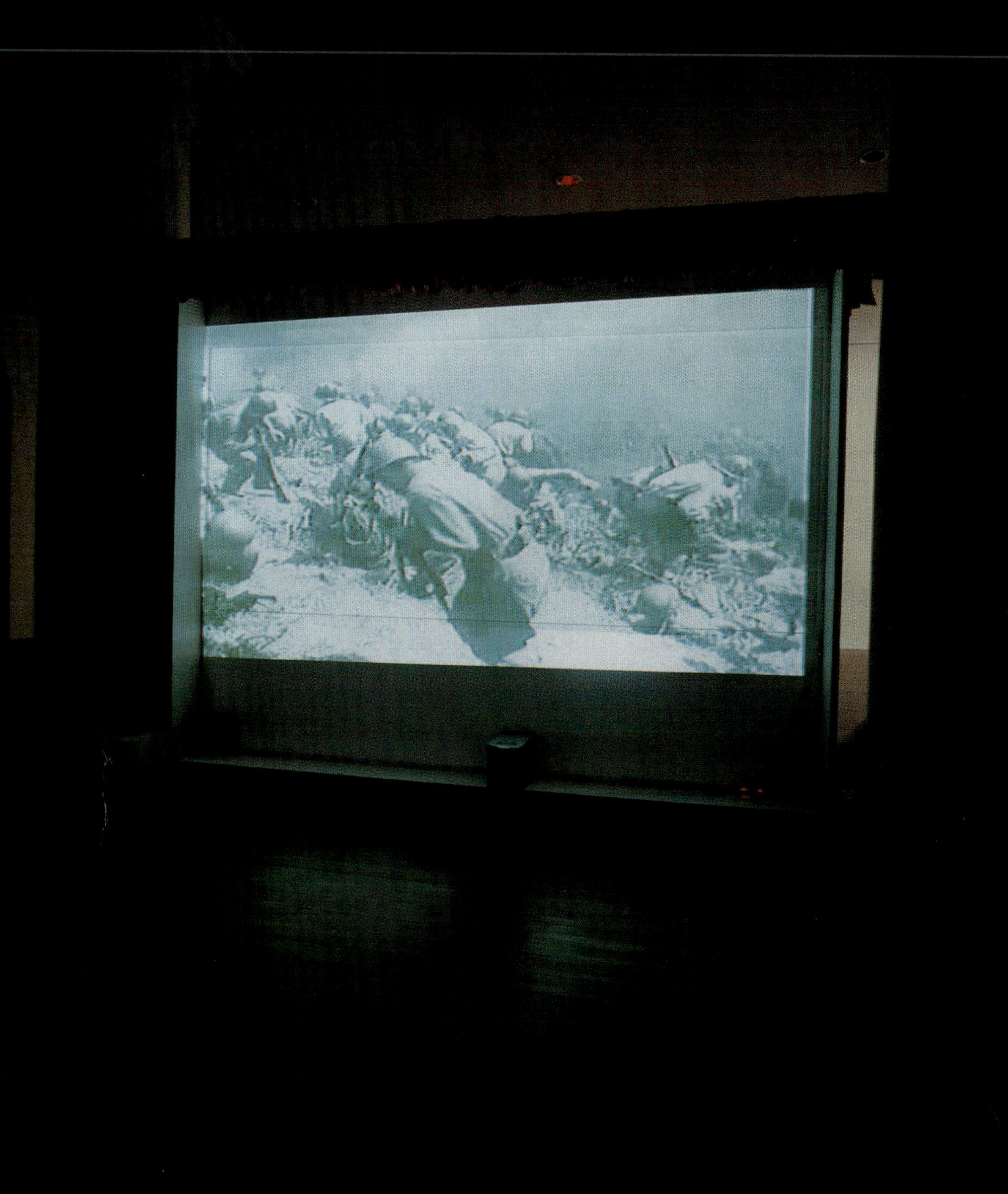

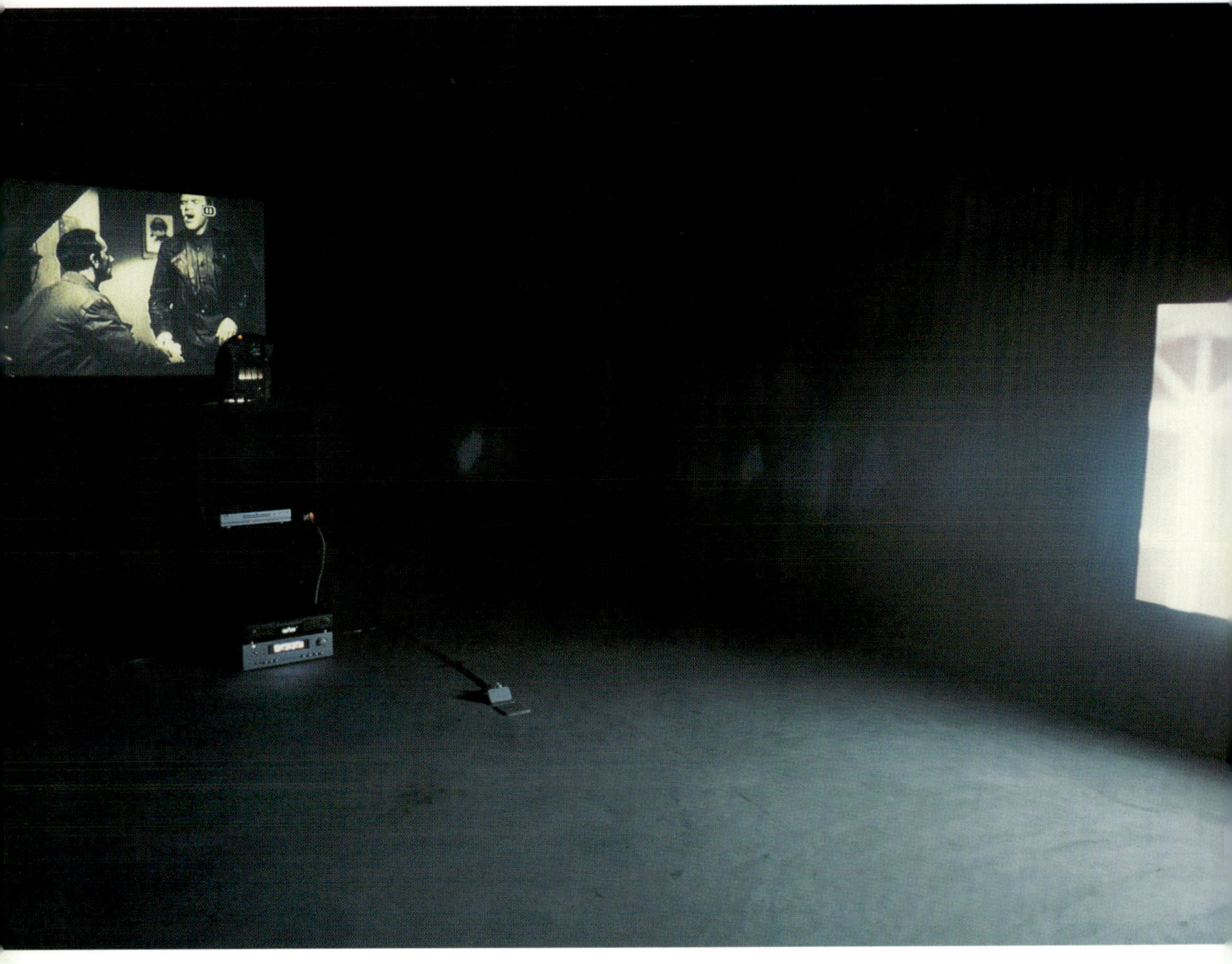

Is He a Traitor? - Post Production

Wang Jianwei, 2002

video projection, soundtrack, photograph on lightbox, dimensions variable, installation at EMAC, Beijing (China), 2002

the artist uses images from the Russian film Lenin in 1918, which applauded the Bolshevik Revolution and was enormously popular in China. Short fragments from the film are assembled and repeated (endlessly). The picture quality of the film varies from scene to scene according to the subjective memory of the artist; for example, some of the images are becoming gradually vague while others are getting sharper. The sound is from a separate CD track, which is synchronized with the images at the beginning but gradually desynchronizes from the images. The sound is a mixture of the film's original soundtrack and other recordings that the artist thinks are related to the film.

布哈林是叛徒吗？ ——后期制作

汪建伟，2002

录像装置，投影机，灯箱照片，声音，可变尺寸，

远洋艺术中心，北京，中国，2002

在《布哈林是一个叛徒？》中艺术家重新编辑了苏联电影《列宁在1918》中的某些片段。每一个场景的画面效果根据艺术家的主观记忆做了不同的处理。声音来自一个独立的音轨。最初，音响与影像同步，但在播放过程中逐渐地相互脱离。当它重复播放到一定程度，又变为同步。

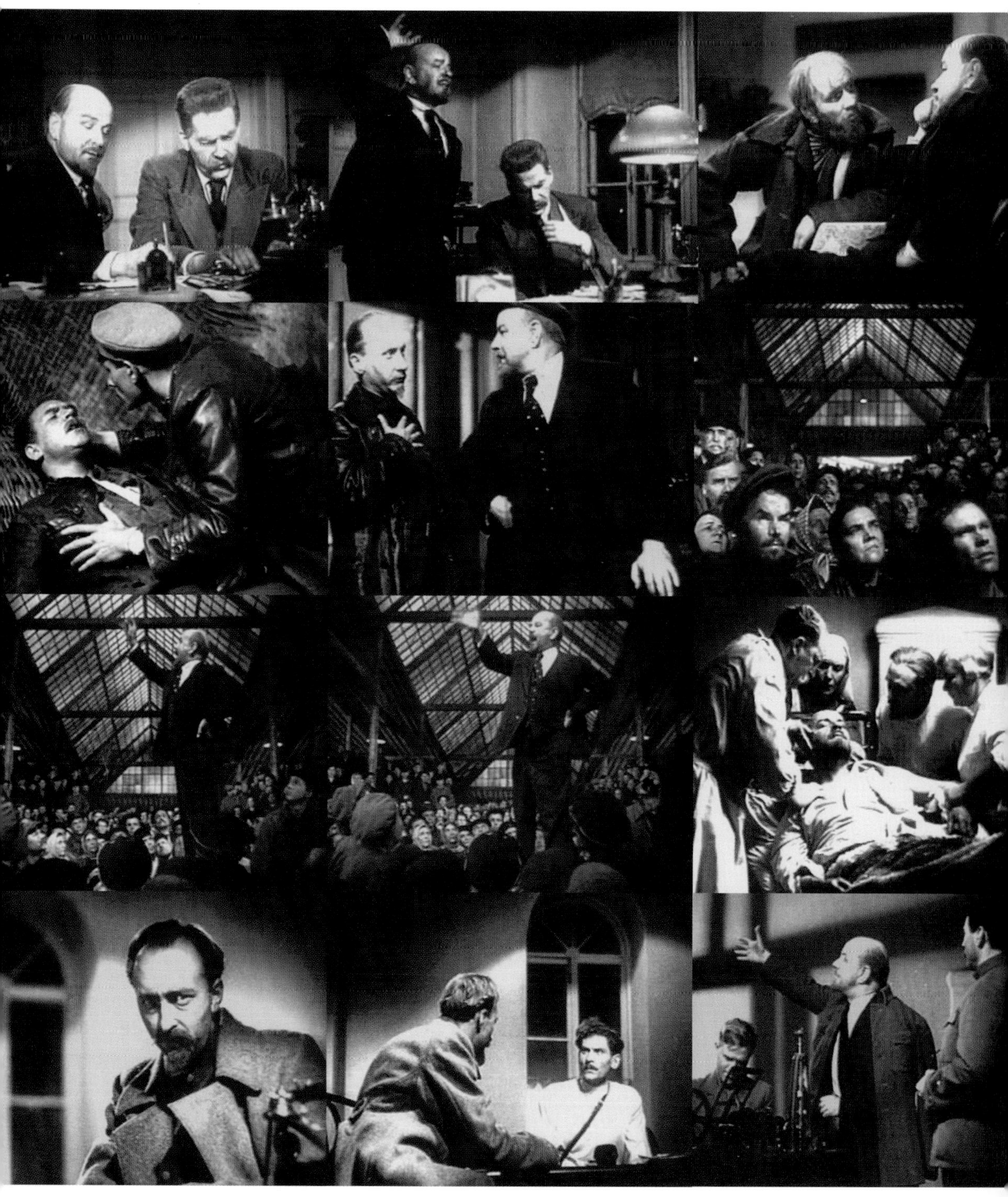

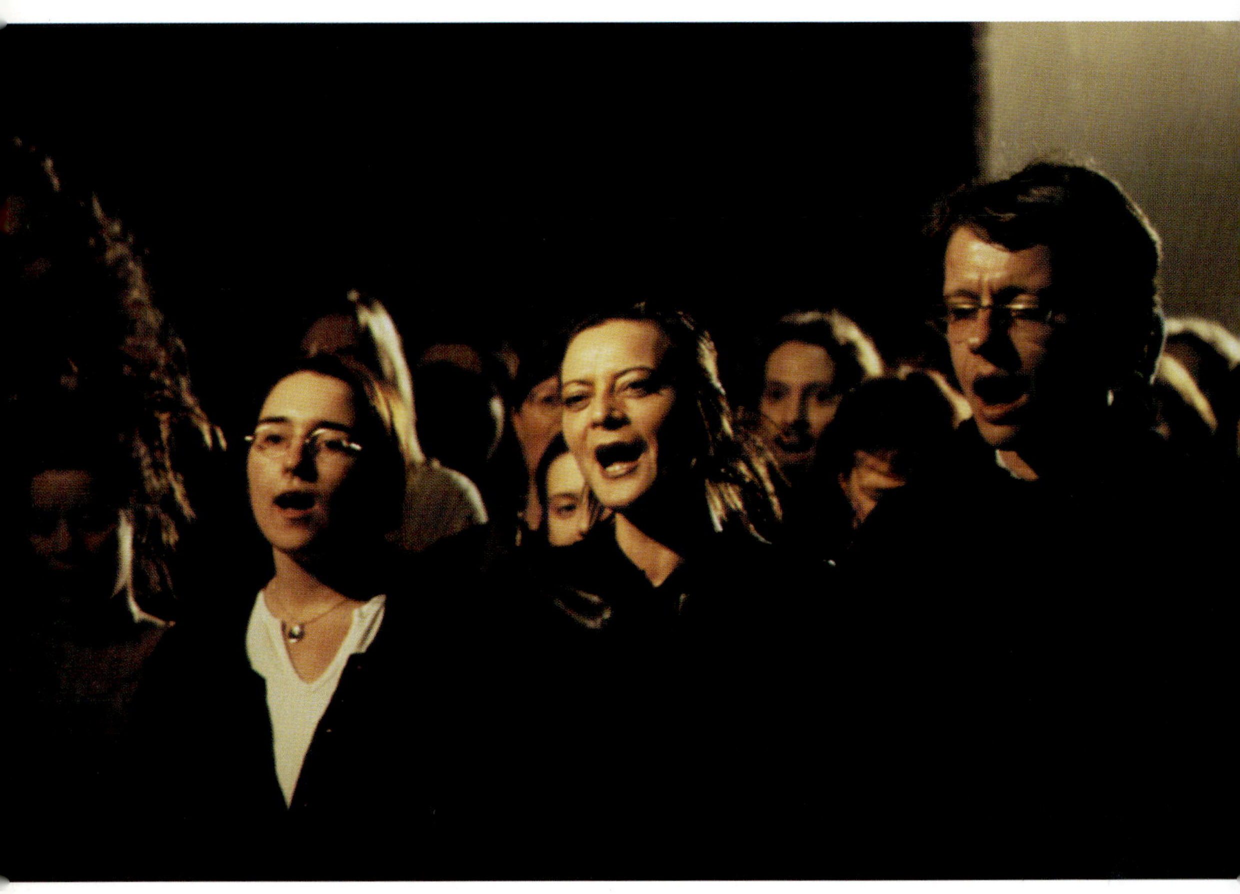

The Hidden Wall

Wang Jianwei, 2001

performance, Haus der Kulturen der Welt, Berlin (Germany), 2001

隐蔽的墙

汪建伟，2001

表演，柏林世界文化宫，德国，2001

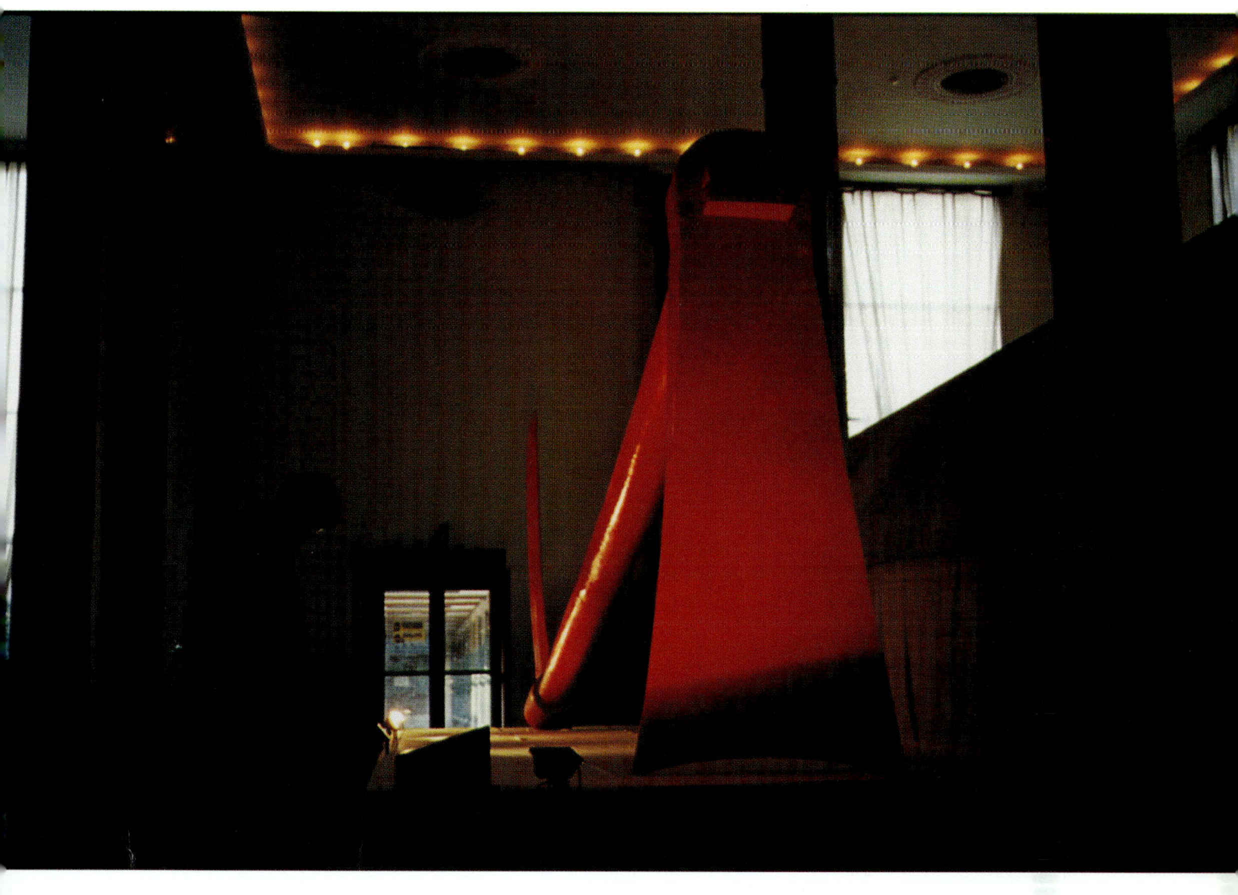

Theater
Wang Jianwei, 2002
installation, Beijing Agricultural
Museum, Beijing (China), 2002

剧场
汪建伟，2002
单视频录像装置
北京农业展览馆，中国，2002

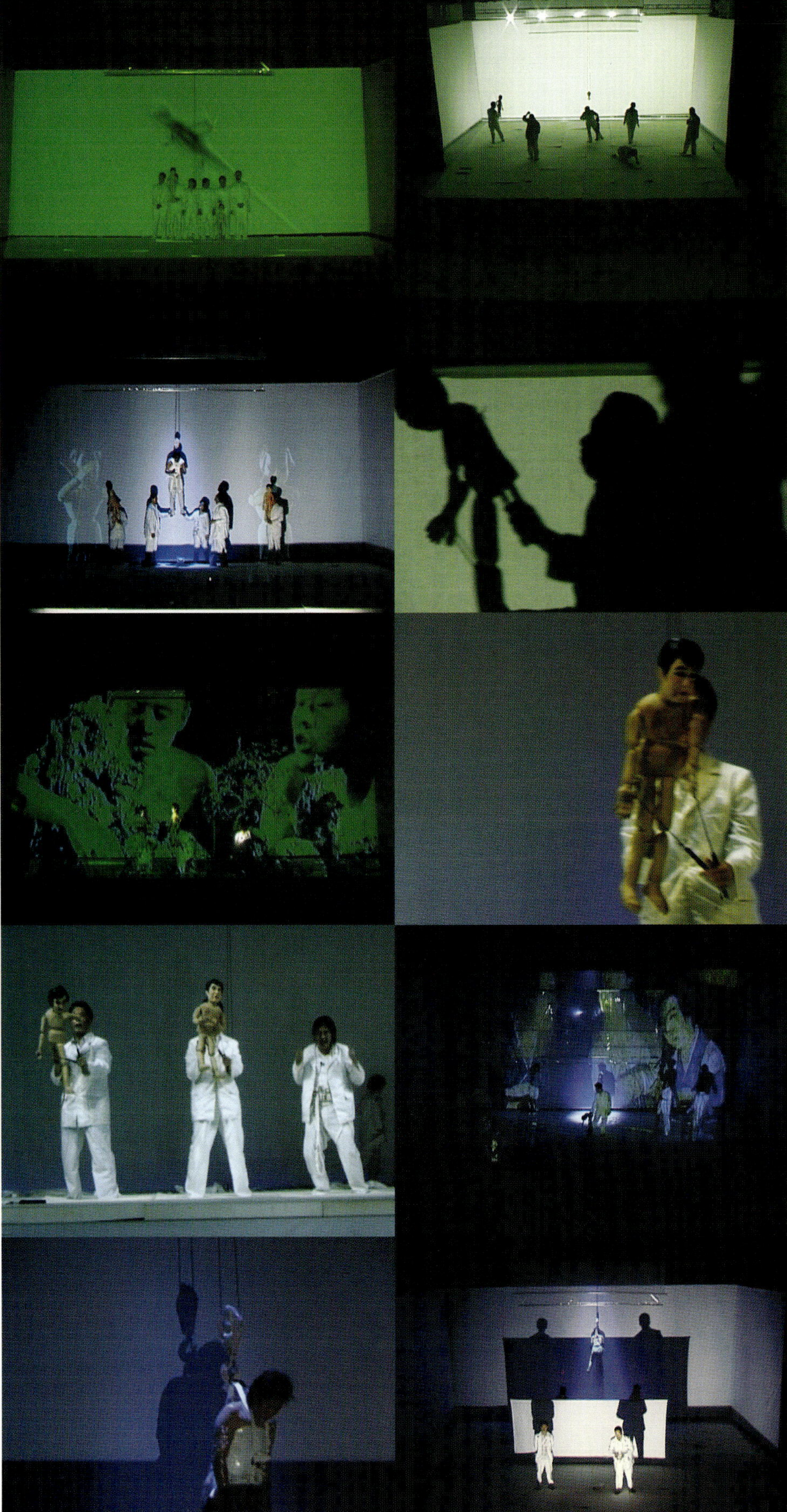

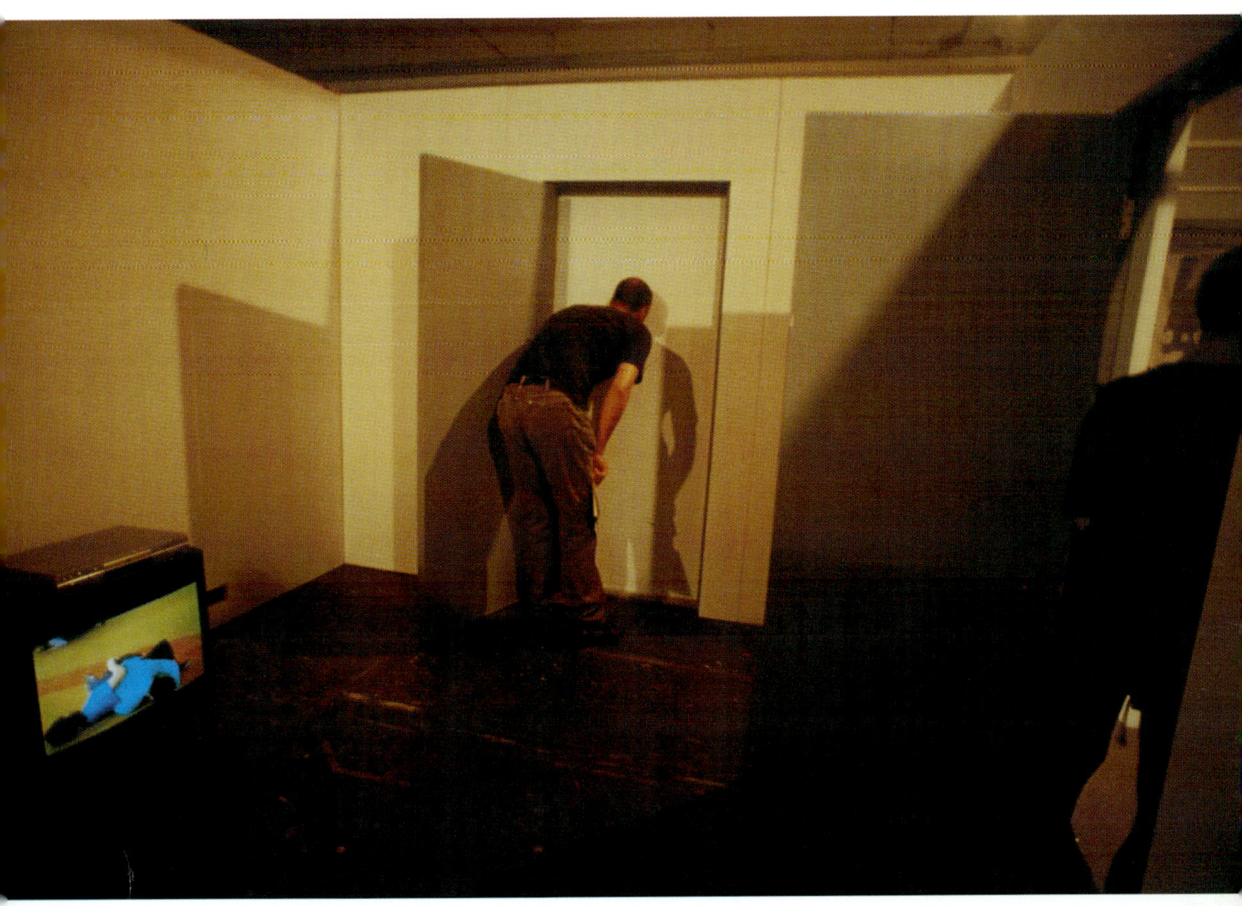

The Screen
Wang Jianwei, 2000
multi-media play and performance, video projection, sound and lighting

屏风
汪建伟，2000
多媒体戏剧

Zhang Peili

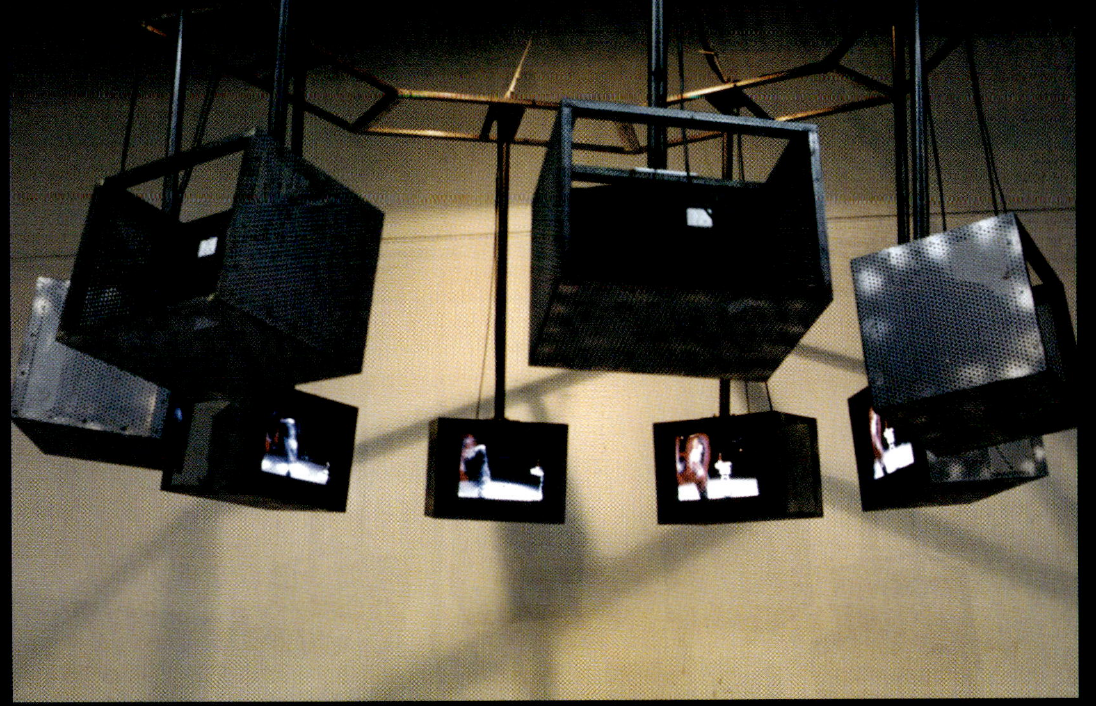

Magic in the Circle

Zhang Peili, 2002

video installation, 8 channels

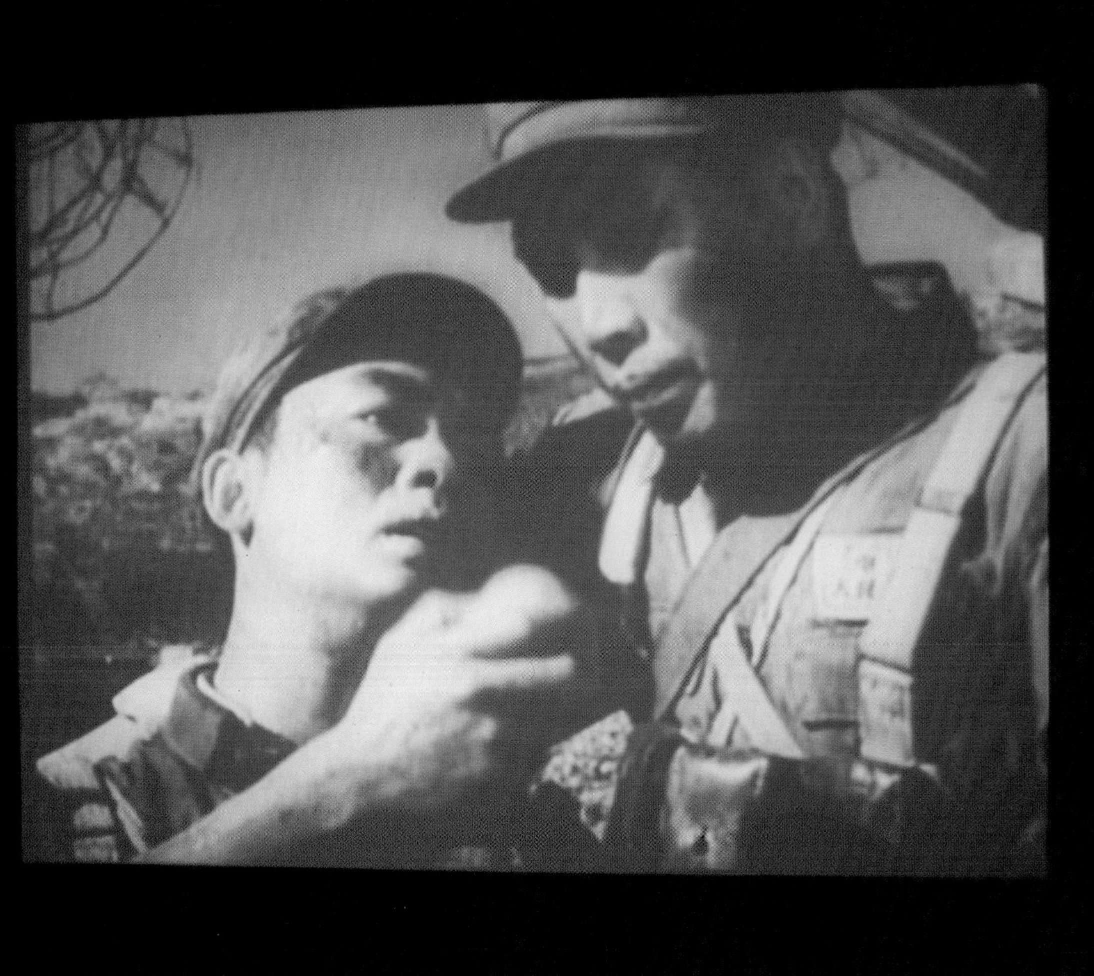

Last Words

Zhang Peili, 2002

video installation, 2 channels, installation at EMAC Beijing (China), 2002

A video compiled of numerous scenes of dying heroes, taken from old Chinese revolutionary movies. The compilation consists two video channels.
One shows the heroes endlessly uttering their last words and dying. The other, a reversed version of the former, shows the heroes reviving.

遗言

张培力 2002

2 视频录像装置，远洋艺术中心，北京，中国，2002

作品综合了中国五六十年代革命影片中英雄牺牲的诸种场景。该装置包括两个录像频道，分别被投映在两个屏幕上。从其中一个屏幕上观众看到无数英雄不断地壮烈牺牲。另一个屏幕则是前一个屏幕影像的倒放，即英雄死而复生。

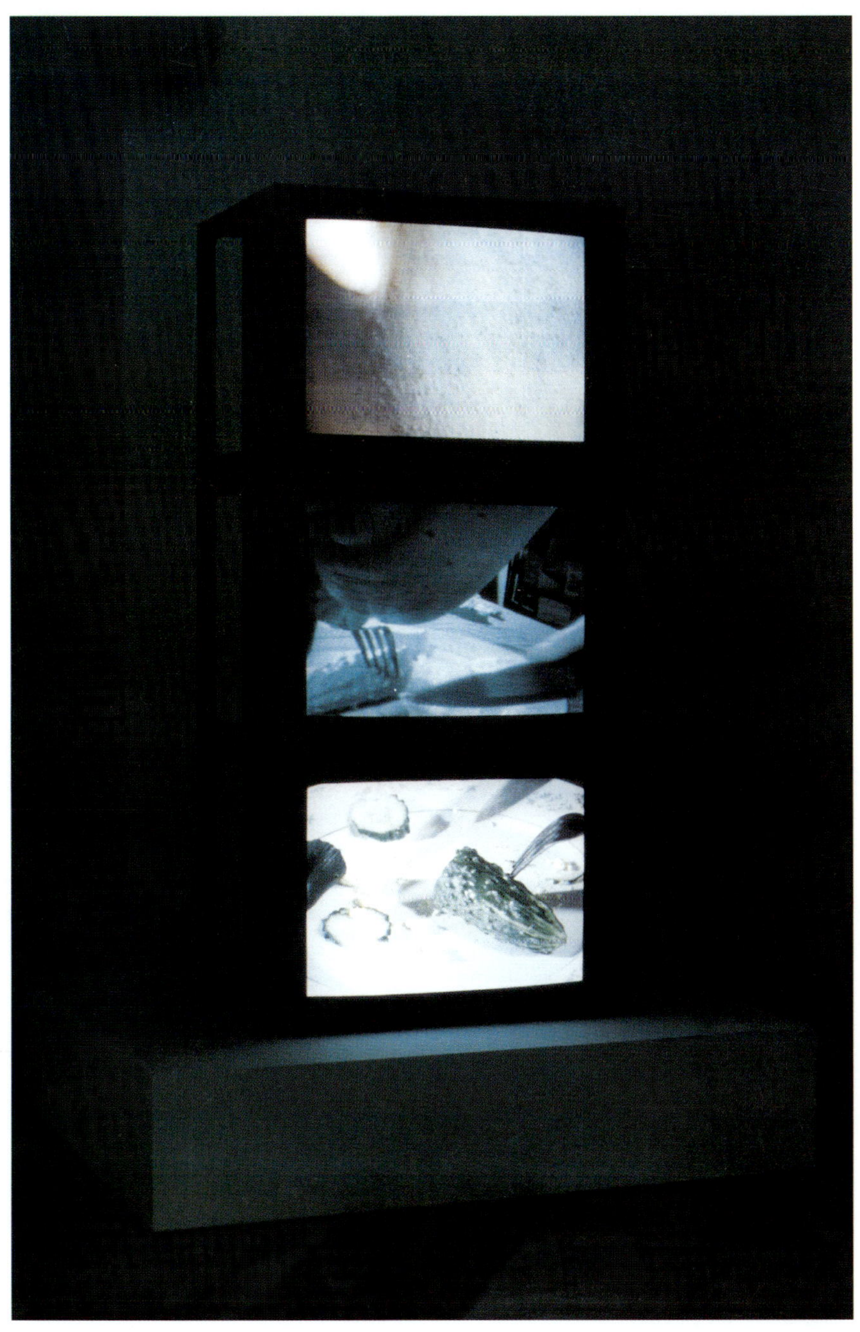

Eating

Zhang Peili, 1997

video installation, 3 channels installtion at the Museum of Modern Art, NewYork (The U.S.A.)1997

The installation consists of three close-up images of a person who is eating.

进食

张培力 1997

3 视频录像装置，纽约现代艺术博物馆，美国

这个录像记录一个人正在咀嚼的三个不同部位的特写。

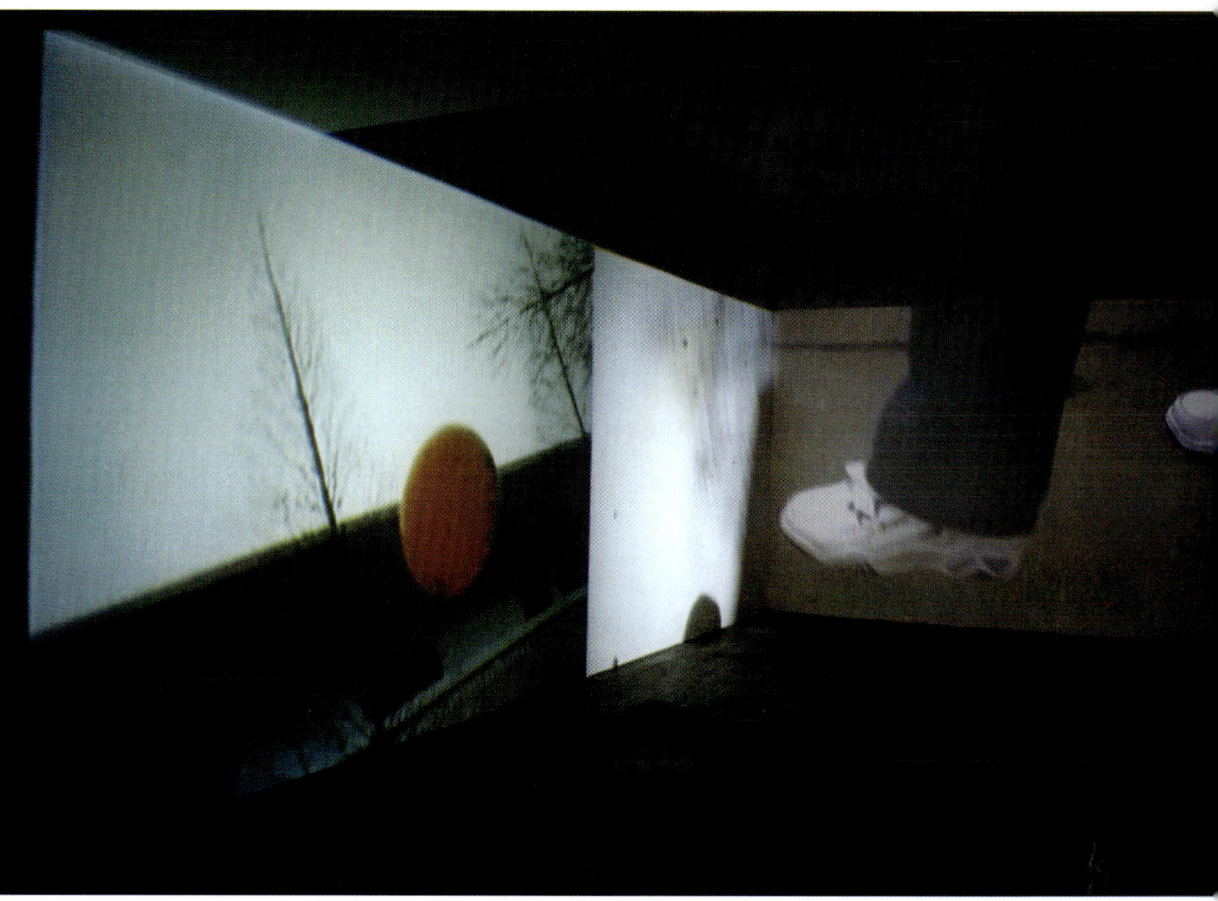

Air

Zhang Peili, 1998

video installation, 3 channels.

The piece consists of three video channels that depict a person playing with a balloon. The video images were shot from three different camera angles and recorded simultaneously. One channel shows the sky recorded from a camera attached to the arm that is striking the balloon upwards and the other follows the balloon. The third channel shows the feet and the steps of the person who is playing with the balloon.

空气

张培力 1998

3 视频录像装置

这一作品由三个视频构成，三台摄像机同时从不同的角度拍摄一个人往空中拍打气球。一个摄像机被绑在那个拍打者的手臂上，画面呈现的是晃动的天空；另一个摄像机跟随着气球起落；第三个摄像机拍摄那个拍打者的双脚。整个作品由三组画面组成，每组画面分别纪录三个不同的表演者拍打气球的行为。

(top) **30 x 30**
Zhang Peili, 1988
single channel video

(below)**Document on "Hygiene" No. 3**
Zhang Peili, 1991
single channel video

30 x 30
张培力 1988
单视频录像

（卫）字 3 号
张培力 1991
单视频录像

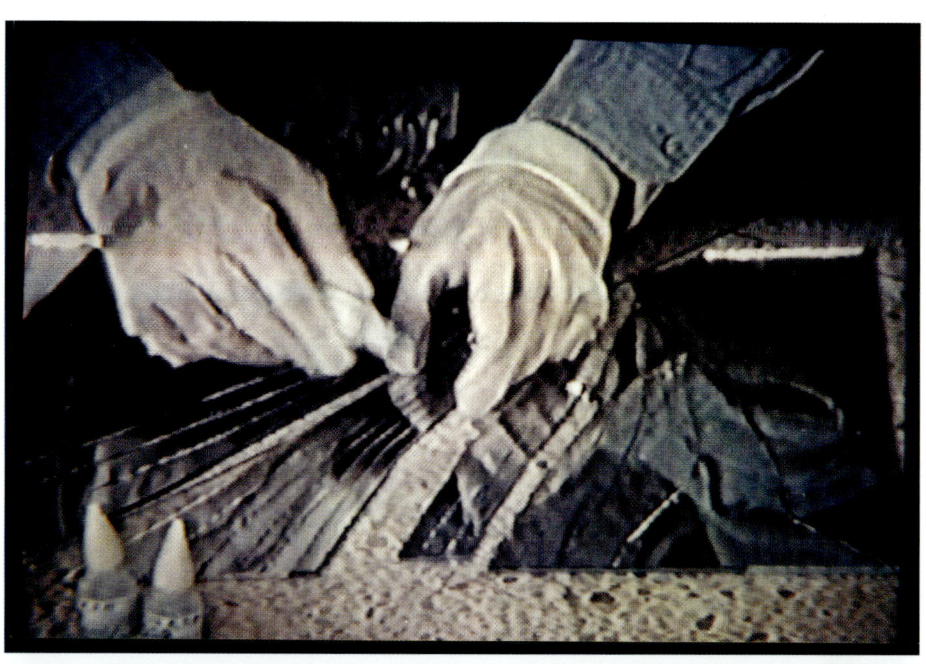

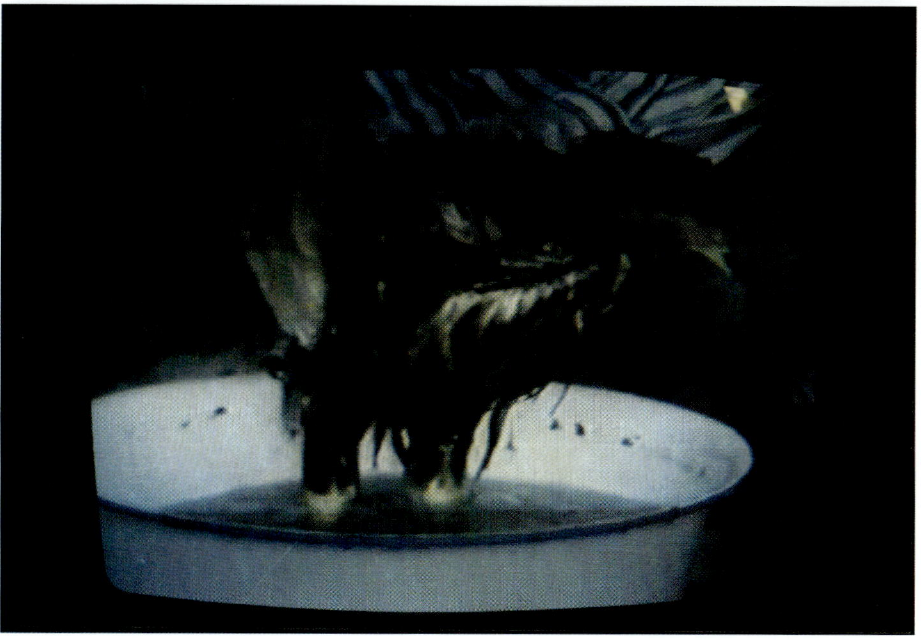

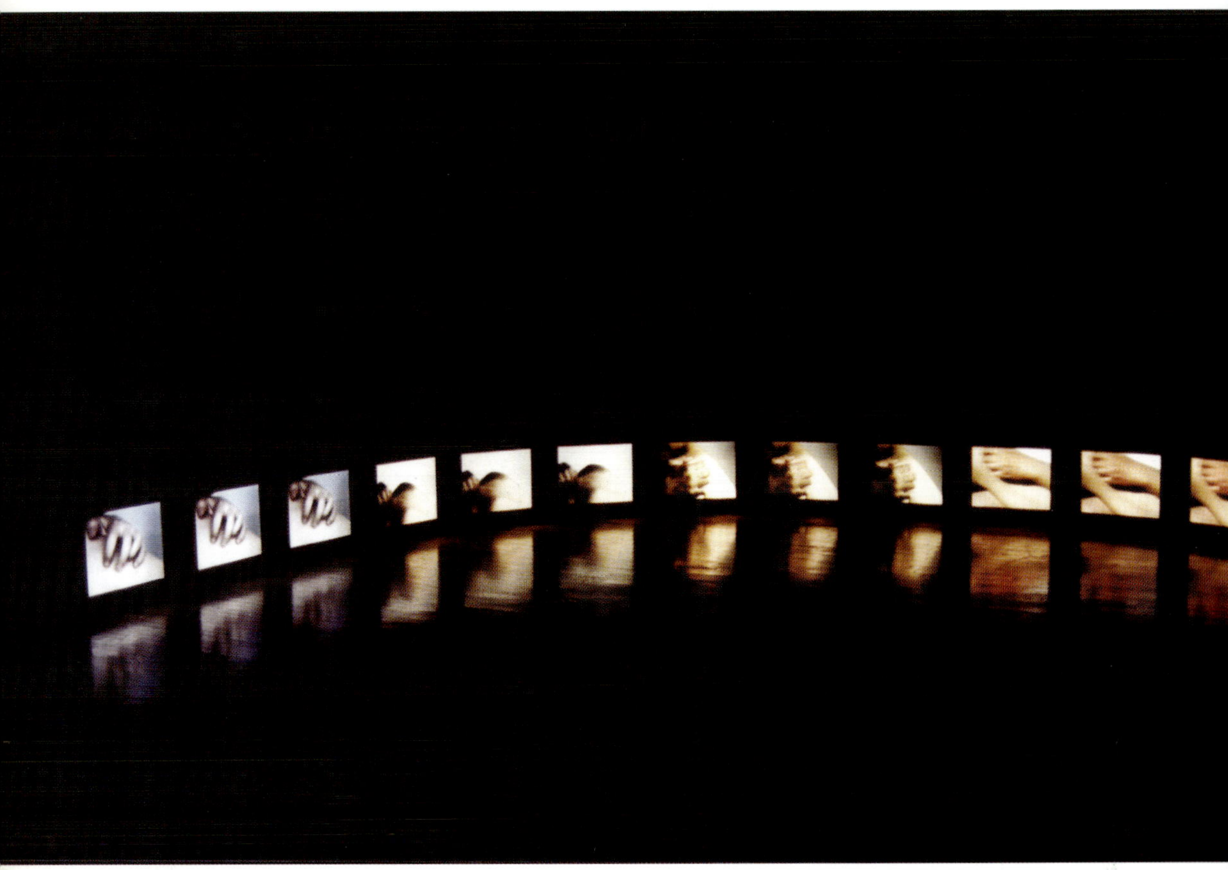

Uncertain Pleasure

Zhang Peili, 1996

video installation, 4 channels, installation at Fukuoka Asian Art Museum (Japan), 1996

A multi-channel installation shows close-up images of a person constantly scratching his body.

不确切的快感

张培力 1996

4 视频录像装置，福冈美术馆，日本，1996

这个多频道的装置展示了这个总在挠痒痒的人的特写。

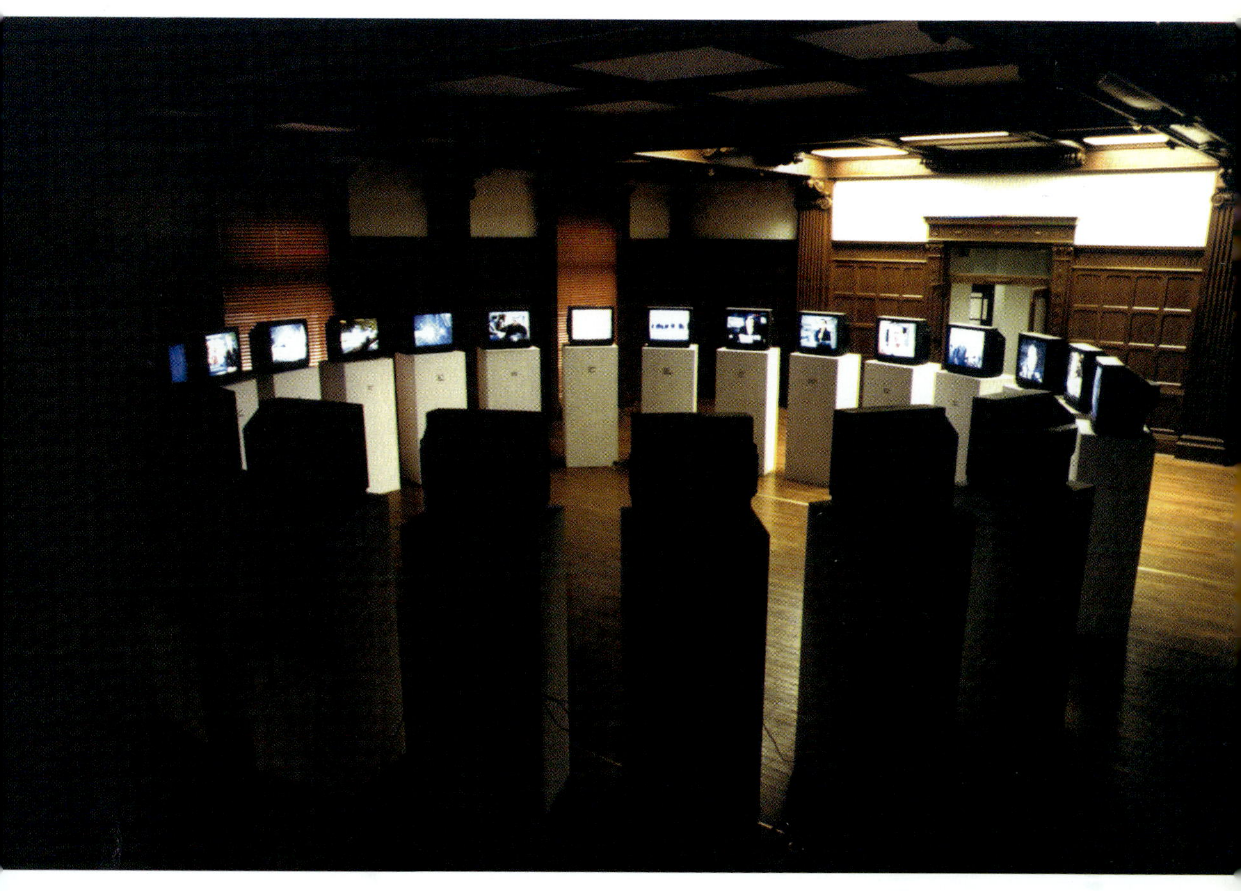

Simultaneous Broadcast

Zhang Peili, 2000

video installation, 23 channels, installation at Shanghai Art Museum (China), 2000

The installation shows 26 news-announcers simultaneously reading the news in different languages.

同时播出

张培力, 2000

23 视频录像装置，上海美术馆，中国

这个装置展现的是 26 位来自世界各地的新闻播音员用不同的语言同时播报新闻。

Zhu Jia

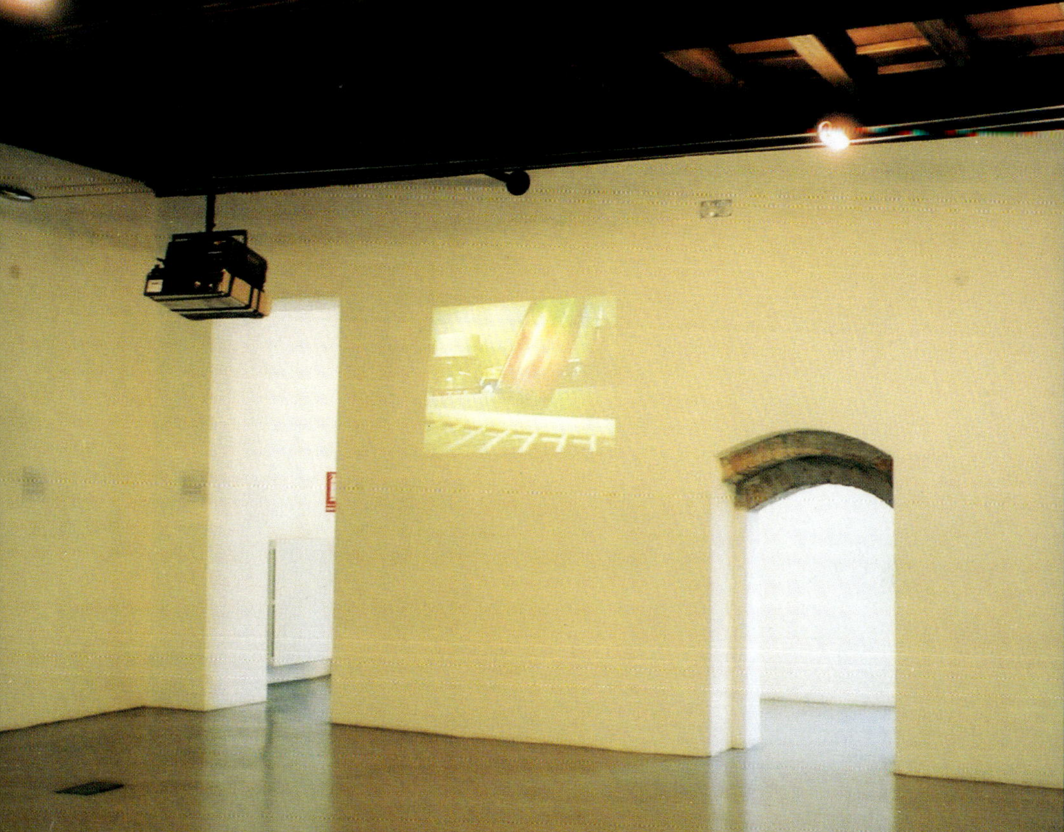

Repeat on Purpose

Zhu Jia, 1997

video, single channel, installation at Castello di Rivoli - Museo d'Arte

Contemporanea, Torino (Italy), 2000

Placed inside a refrigerator and facing the refrigerator door, the camera records the deliberate
repetition of opening and closing the refrigerator.

刻意的重复

朱加，1997

单视频录像装置，Castell di Rivori 当代艺术博物馆，都灵，意大利，2000

将摄像机放在冰箱内，镜头对着冰箱门，摄像机纪录重复开关冰箱门的过程。

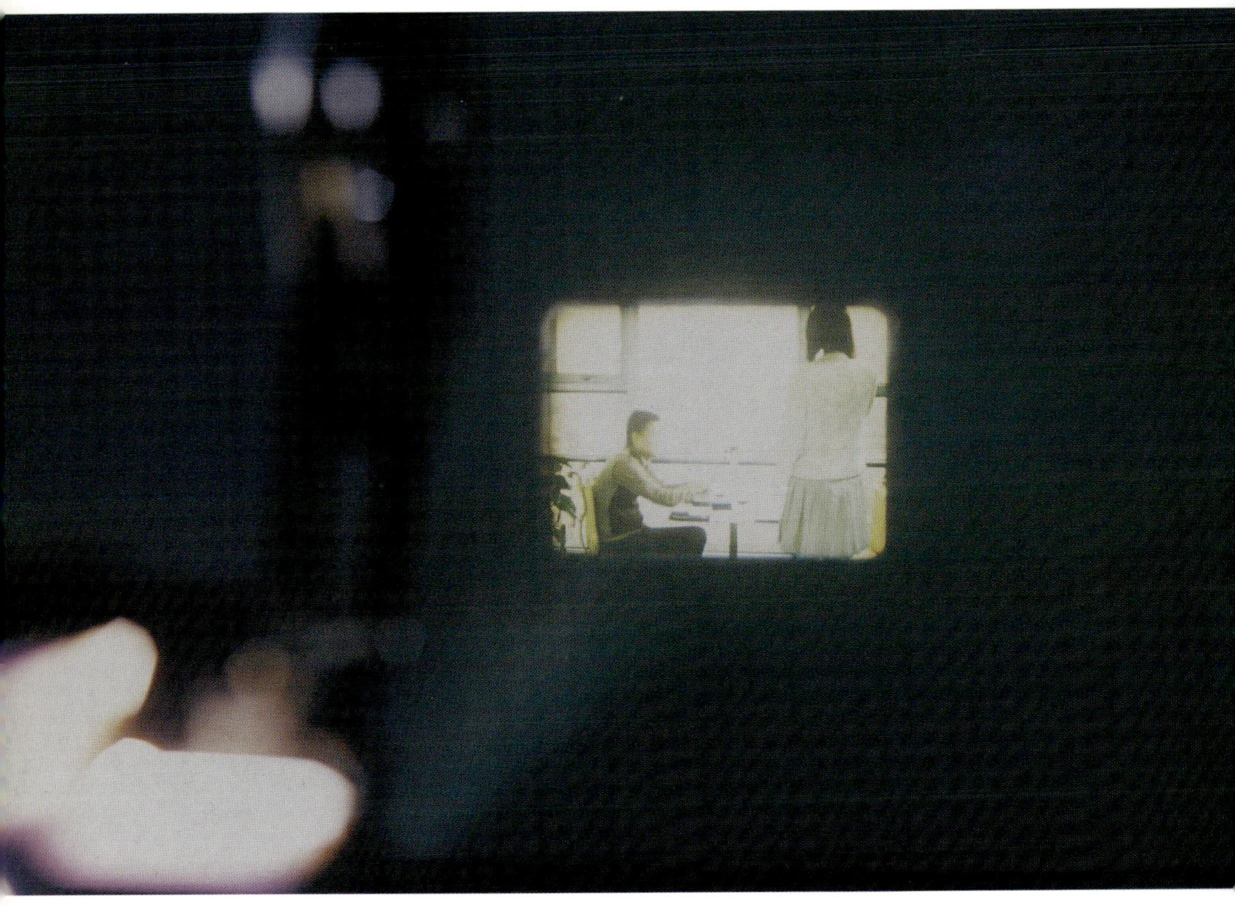

Double Landscape

Zhu Jia, 2002

16 mm film projection, installation at EMAC, Beijing (China), 2002

The film shows a young man drinking coffee in front of a window through which the landscape of a modern city can be seen. A lady, standing motionless, seems to be serving the man. Although it is difficult to realize for the viewer, she is actually a dressed mannequin.

双重风景

朱加，2002

16毫米电影、远洋艺术中心、北京、中国、2002

影像记录一个年轻男子坐在窗前喝咖啡，一看似真人的衣架模特儿背对观众。窗外是城市风景。

本片由固定机位拍摄。

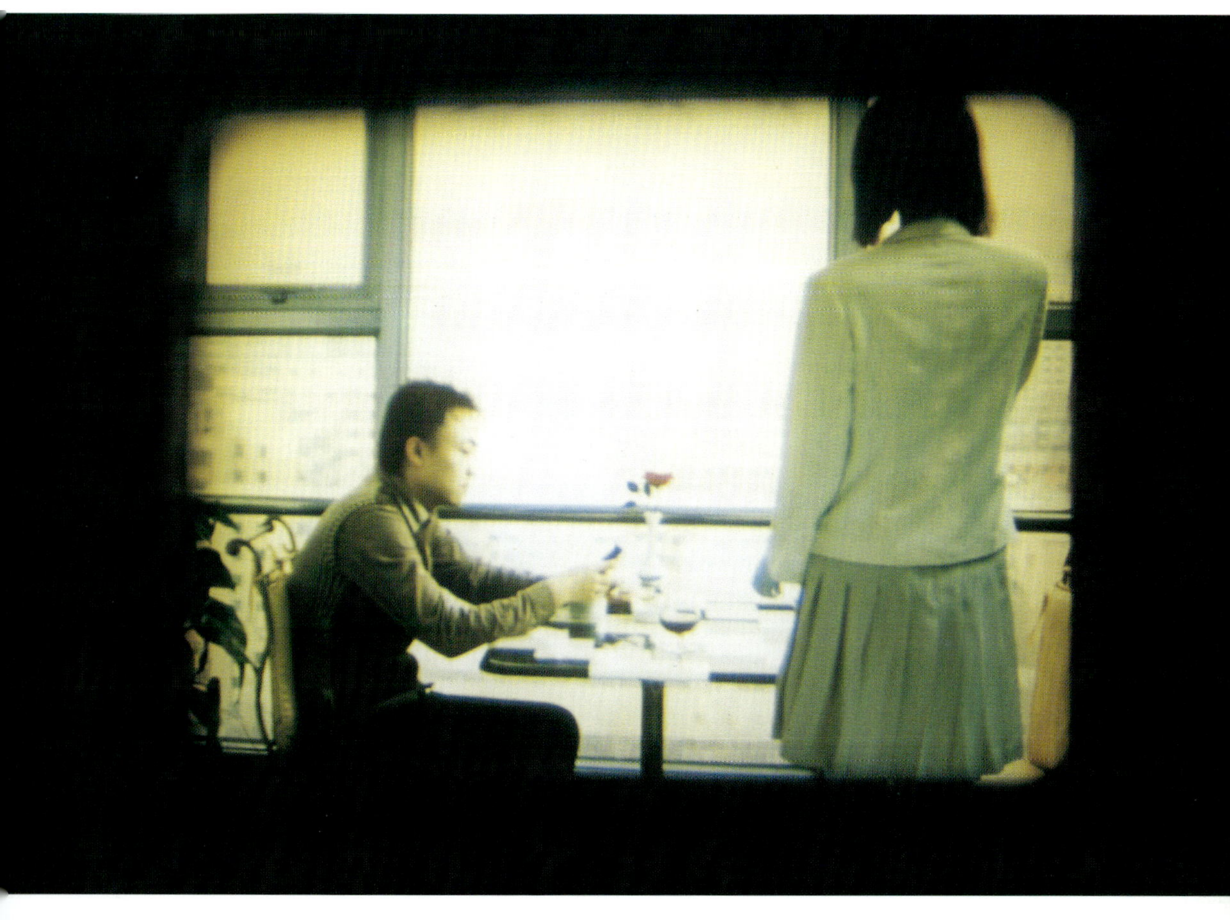

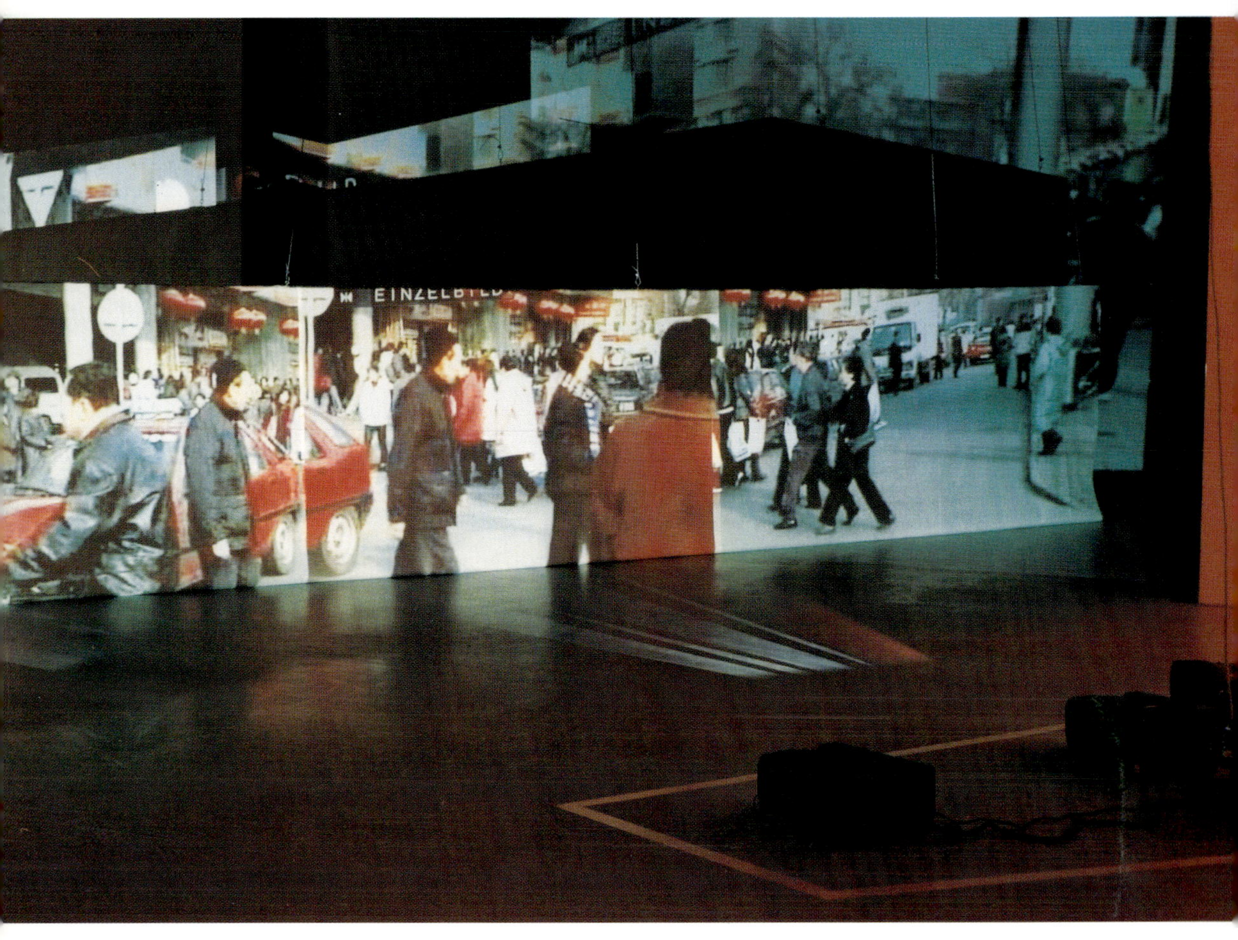

Linked Scenery

Zhu Jia, 2000

video installation, 3 channels, sound, installation at Haus der Kultüren der Welt, Berlin (Germany), 2001

连接的风景

朱加，2000

3 视频录像装置，声音，柏林世界文化宫，德国，2001

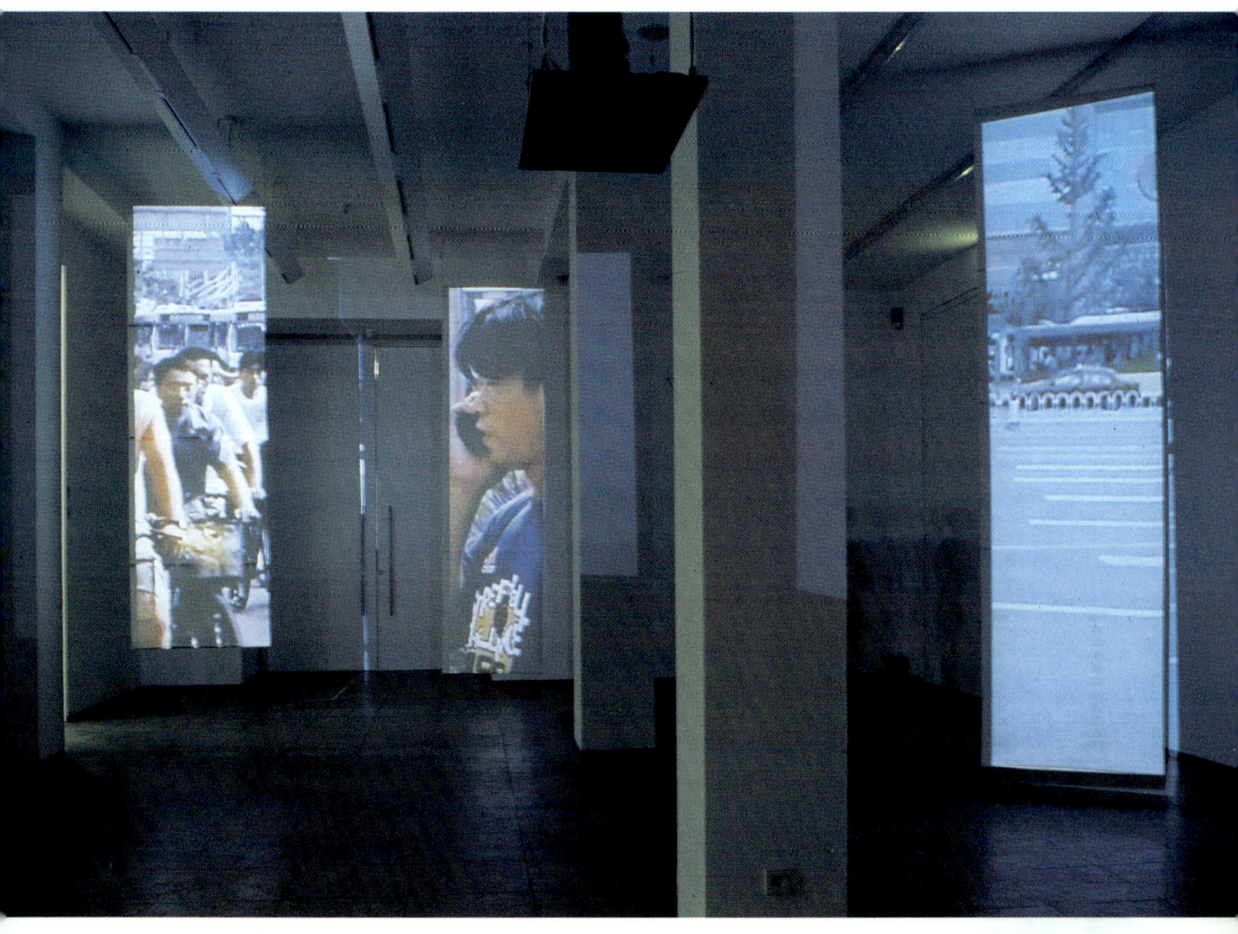

Passage
Zhu Jia, 2001
installation, video projection, 3 channels, single soundtrack, dimensions variable,
installation at Nationalgalerie im Hamburger Bahnhof
Museum fur Gegenwart - Berlin (Germany), 2001

通道
朱加，2001
3视频录像装置，单声道，可变尺寸，汉堡火车站美术馆，柏林，德国，2001

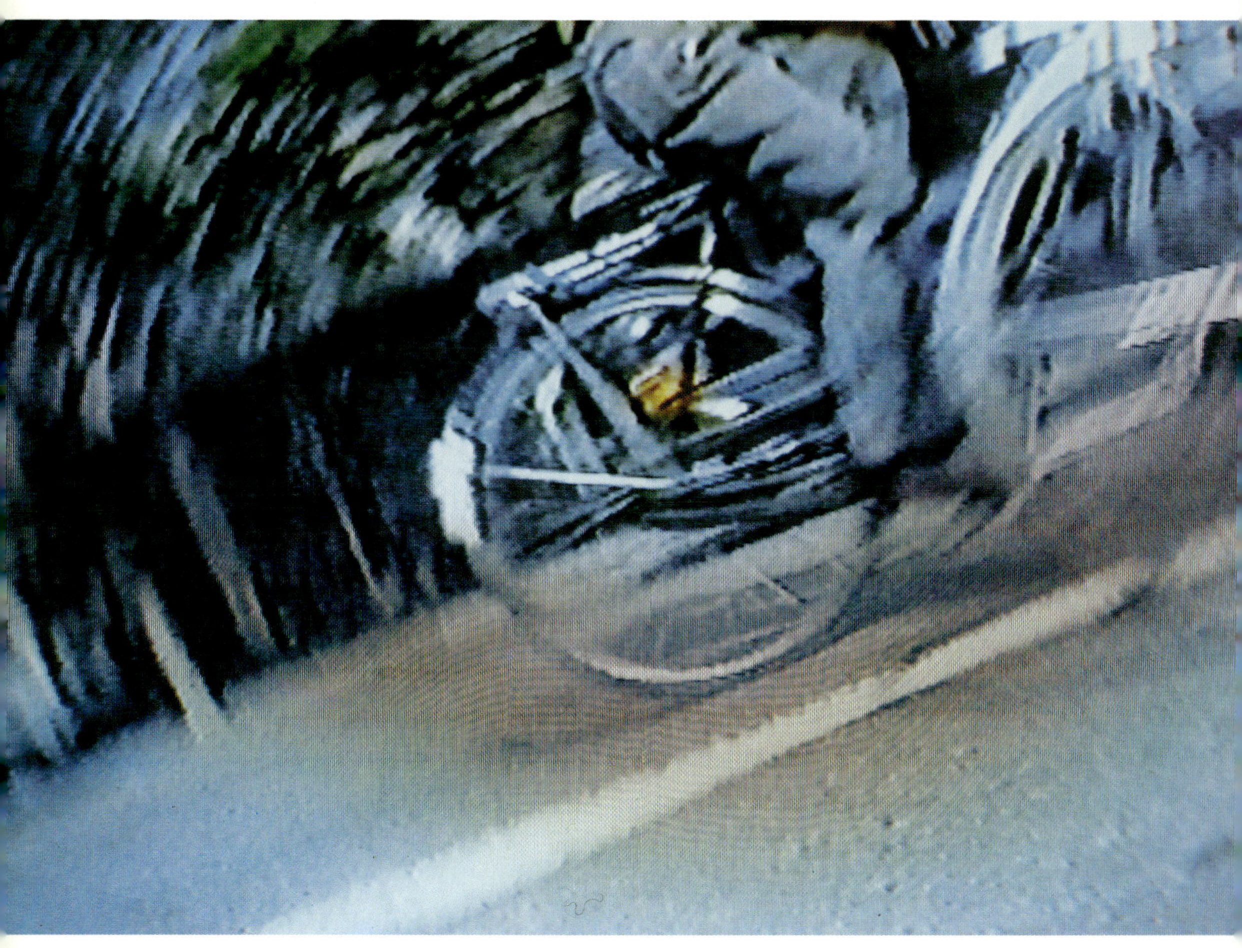

Forever

Zhu Jia, 1994

video, single channel, no sound, 30 minutes

*The images result from a camera attached to the left
wheel of a tricycle which the artist rode though the
streets of Beijing for 30 minutes during the process
of recording. The video is unedited.*

不停止

朱加，1994

单视频录像，无声，30分钟

将摄像机绑在一辆三轮车的左侧轮子上，镜头朝外，开
启摄录键，在北京的街道上骑行30分钟。这个录像是
以这样的方式拍下来的，无任何编辑。

Related to Environmen

Zhu Jia, 1997

video installation, single channel, sound

installation at Golden Island, Sydney (Australia), 1998

与环境有关

朱加，1997

单视频录像装置，同期声，循环播放，黄

金岛，悉尼，澳大利亚，1998

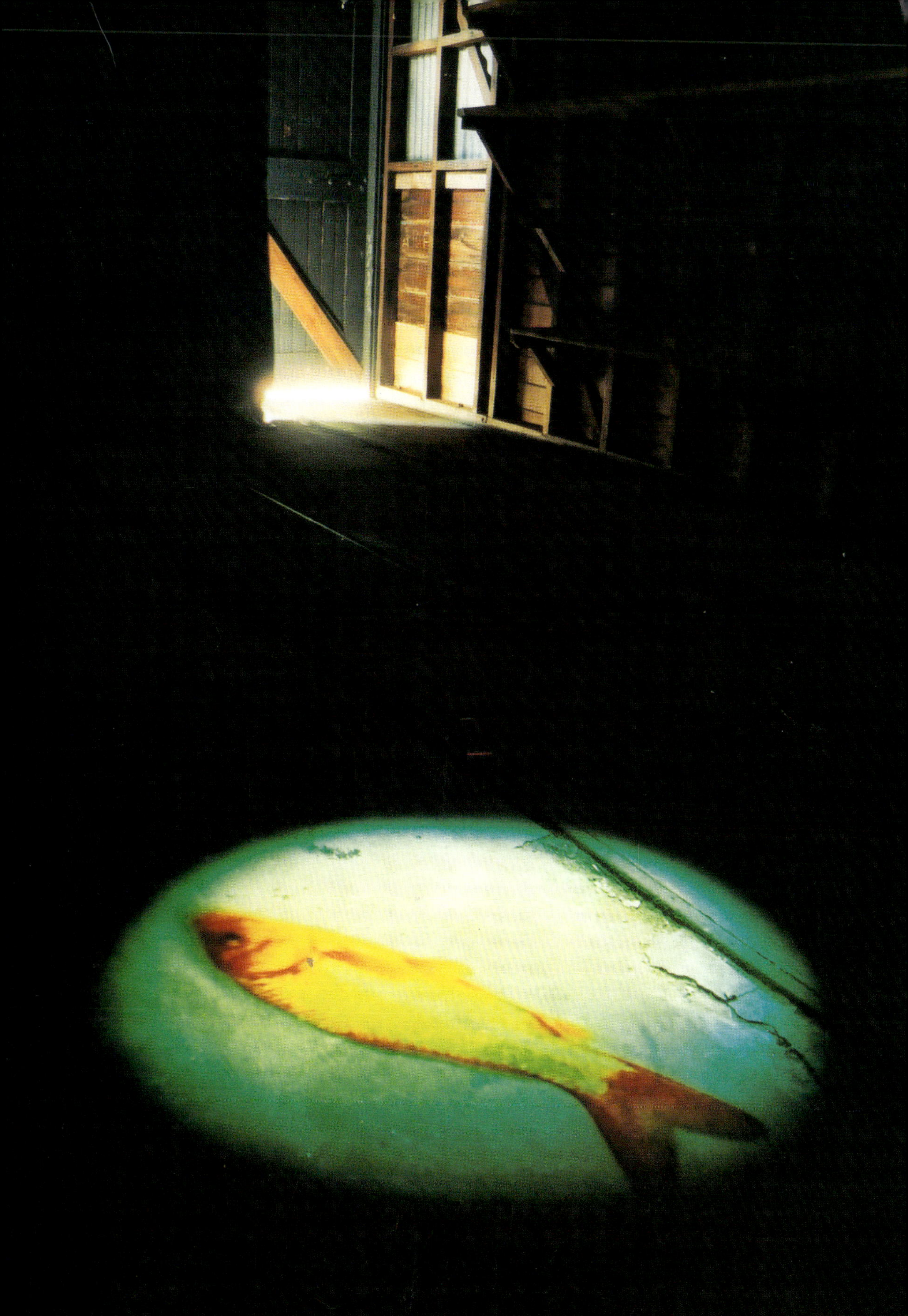

声西击东

Marianne Brouwer

这是一个来自八十年代中期的故事：一位移民到巴黎的中国年轻艺术家去见赵无极。这个年轻的艺术家问赵无极：要在西方开创事业他该做些什么。赵无极告诉他："不要再说一句中文，不要与任何中国人交谈，完全忘记你是中国人。然后，你就有可能会在西方成功"。

在那个时代这样的态度是很平常的。例如，谁会在乎超现实主义画家 Wilfredo Lam 本是古巴人，或概念艺术家 Stanley Brouwn 来自苏里南国？即使现代艺术起源于西方，那并不妨碍他们的作品成为现代艺术的一部分，我们看见的仅仅是百分之百的国际主义艺术。对于有些人，这种论调涉及到现代艺术批评的潜在可能性，关系到其革命性源头达达主义、未来主义和结构主义，而对于另一些人则关系到作为自发性艺术的现代主义纯粹价值(value free)。事实上，各种事件所呈现的是一种心理状态，但整个形势在七十年代中期开始变化。新一代艺术家已经诞生，

这些人中很多人是难民——譬如说我回忆起南美洲流放艺术家带来的第一次冲击波；另外一些艺术家出生在别处——大都是在前殖民国家——他们到西方来学习；还有一些出生于移民家庭。他们有一种完全不同于西方艺术家的态度，即呼吁关注他们作品中的非西方因素和其政治上的重要性。在非西方国家工作的当代艺术家们很快加入到他们的阵营，中国艺术家也在其中。但是，一方面在于过去十年，越来越多的移民和难民涌进西方国家，另一方面由于9.11事件的后果，多重文化主义的上升趋势逐渐被强硬的移民法、警察条例以及政治倾斜所遏制，不断增加并流行的外国人恐惧症情绪刺激了这些法规的制定。随着全世界的国际性展览数量逐渐增多，再反衬着日益成功并有声望的"全球性"艺术，这些规章制度显得格外生硬。

要理解在过去十年中国当代艺术在西方如此成功的原因，我们不得不记住时代的上下文关系：在中国文化大革命结束以及其后的政治变化；国际上，柏林墙的倒塌；全球化经济的建构以及中国作为未来经济超级力量的崛起。以上这些都标志着一个新纪元的来临。

1989年在巴黎蓬皮杜中心举办的展览《大地魔术师》，象征性地标志着当代艺术全球化的到来。西方艺术界第一次与来自全球的当代艺术谋面，三个中国艺术家参展，他们是黄咏焙，杨洁昌和顾德新。其结果是，中国似乎一夜之间便跻身于当代艺术中。仅仅几年以后，1992年着陆于欧洲的巡回展《中国前卫艺术》获得空前的成功。此展览是对中国当代艺术的首次概述，是一次相当内行的抉择，展示了大量的90年代生活在中国或海外的中国艺术家的作品。这个内行的评定主要来自汉斯·凡·代克。此人是一个荷兰画廊老板，艺术爱好者，他生活在中国大约25年，一直不懈地支持中国当代艺术。巡回展后，我们突然间发现，中国艺术不再意味着传统或社会主义现实主义。一种新的艺术现象在文化大革命之后一直处于不断的发展之中。

85新潮艺术变成了装置艺术、观念艺术、政治波普等等，并且，这种艺术在使用西方习语的同时从"碎片中"找到了某种适合于它自身的东西。这种艺术毋庸置疑是中国的，而且与我们从前所见的有很大的差异。在89年前后，相当一部分艺术家和批评家离开了中国，显而易见，这种艺术在中国官方得不到认可。从那时起，中国当代艺术分成两条线发展：国内的和海外的。在国内

的艺术家奋争获得展览作品的机会,同时还要引起任何一个正在走动的策划人和收藏家的注意;而海外的艺术家制造的中国热已相继出现在双年展、三年展和许多别的展览上。移民到西方的艺术家和批评家废寝忘食地工作,他们同时要在两个相互矛盾的阵线上努力奋斗:为了中国当代艺术在西方和在中国获得认可。我在这里特别指陈箴、黄咏虫、蔡国强、谷文达、杨洁苍以及批评家侯翰如和费大为。陈箴喜欢使用来自著名的"三十六计"的句子作为他的作品的标题,有时候改换个别字词以适合他自己的计划。因此他颠倒了第六计"声东击西",成了"声西击东"。他想要表明,通过在西方成名,中国艺术家们可以奋力促使当代艺术在中国的合法化。另一个陈箴的名言是:"中国艺术家生活在西方就像带有两种文化,两个图书馆,两个军队"。这意味着在海外的中国艺术家肩负着让西方观众理解他们的艺术作品的重任,即为西方翻译中国。自80年代起,在大部分生活在西方的非西方艺术家的作品中,"翻译"已经成为主要问题之一。我认为不幸的是它并没有获得它本应获得的理论上的关注,因为西方批评家根本不知道那是什么意思,也就是说他们不理解随之而来的那些问题。西方有其自身的艺术表达与传播系统。它通常相信——此系统是唯一可行的系统模式。如果一个艺术作品要被解释成艺术家的所指,他或她不得不创造一个上下文关系或翻译系统,利用变换的,同时很可能是相反的文化时态使这些作品的存在可以被阅读和理解。但是理解也许并不是真正的目的(我猜测),错读和误读是西方接受"他者文化"的一个"有机部分"。但人们似乎并不关心这些,只要这个艺术家很出名,简言之,像一个"战利品"。例如,1994年在我策划的展览《暗黑之心》中,蔡国强计划在博物馆四围拔起一定数量的树木,重新把它们倒过来栽种。一个批评家按字面意义把它理解为"无根",即无家园和流放的意思。事实上此作品演示了道家关于治理国家的脱节或骚乱的观念:通过停止和颠倒时间。因倒载的树能够从树冠上生根,且继续生长,这似乎是个众所周知的现象。

我在前文里提到的关于赵无极和那个焦急的学生的故事也许有助于描绘一个巨大的裂缝。此裂缝存在于在80年代世界其他地方"蒸蒸日上"的现代艺术与西方现代艺术之间。它足已阐明此裂缝是起因于艺术界所固有的关于什么是现代艺术以及现代艺术应该是怎样的概念。也就是说:处于一种积极的表述需求与对在世界其它地区所发生的现代主义的不可理解性之间的裂缝。换句话说,在西方的眼中,现代艺术曾经等于"西方"。这种观点的后果之一是通过西方的眼睛满足对"东方的"不同的艺术的偷窥嗜好。"言论自由"是启蒙时代以来西方社会的独一无二的历史性成就这一概念本身直接导致一个反向推理:所有来自受压抑国家(例如俄国或中国)的艺术必须是带有 DISSIDENT 的色彩,如此才能显示其"正宗性"。

这种观点并不能归于任何一类对俄国和中国当代艺术的正确理解。正好相反,像我正要讨论的两者都不能使用西方当代艺术运动的理解方式。西方的理论家、批评家、艺术界有一种偏好,即忽略或抹去独立艺术的深层意义,简单地把"非民主国家"等同于独裁横蛮。但是,所谓的DISSDENT ART 的喧嚣引出了一个怪异的状况:有一段时间,一些想要挣钱的中国艺术家,只要将他们的作品标榜为来自中国的 DISSIDENT 的绘画,"奔驰车"就会停靠在被翻弄一新的胡同前面。这些展览是由保守的画廊和艺术收藏家支持的,既有西方的也有中国的,他们愿意把他们的钞票投资到那样的绘画中,而不是笨重的装置中或任何一种其它的智性的艺术里,这是非常典型的。尽管,作为 DISSIDENT ART 分类之一部分的政治波普倍受赞赏,但它在西方成功的关键不能归应于他的内容而得归应于它是油画，因此再现了传统的、历史的和材料的价值。

一旦"持不同政见"在将来的东方阵营不再是个论点将会怎样，1989年后俄国所发生的也许正好可作为一个将来的研究的例案。柏林墙倒塌以后，著名的嘉士得拍卖行决定主持一次拍卖，内容是莫斯科的新思维(Perestroika)绘画。国际买主云集这个拍卖活动，作品被卖成天价——这可以说成是拍卖行的巨大成功。也可以说在此事件之后的一段时期，俄罗斯独一无二的本土的当代艺术生产的积极部分消失贻尽。很多年里，俄罗斯艺术家在他们的作品中发展了一套有意味的编码，设法规避审查制度。国际艺术商人们和投资者对绘画的内容并不感兴趣。俄国艺术家们原以为他们通过长期斗争才公之于众的论点，能够受到西方的尊重和赞赏，此刻他们才理解到实质上他们是遭到窃掠。我认为，在近来的俄国艺术中，一些富于侵略性的现象溯自那个年代存在着的一种不可见的或无能为力的情感经验。

如果 DISSIDENCE 在这个文本式的游戏中是个主要的论点，东方主义是——并且很长时间以来一直是一个有着"深厚根基"的论点。基本上它有着两种不同的外表。西方对中国当代艺术的期望，即它必定符合一种延续性，至少是在形式上符合中国自身的历史演进。否则，什么是中国的?另一方面，西方批评家们已经对近来中国的装置艺术和影像作品很失望——，这一失望代表的是头一种失望的另一付面孔。特别是，影像艺术使用所谓的"西方的"技术，因此它被认为是相对无趣的，甚至是机会主义的。当然，有时这种艺术的确隐藏着其要出口到西方的目的。正如某些艺术家的确在把玩西方对异国情调的期许。认为影像或别的其他艺术形式所再现的忽略了中国的实际境遇，从某种程度上说明了西方艺术批评家缺乏应有的判断力。另外，我们发现更多的原则性的因素在于西方艺术理论考虑的是艺术自律性。这种前现代主义的自律观不可能是现代性的同义词，因为它把艺术几乎当成是先验性的纯粹价值，独立于社会的、政治的、经济的，甚至文化上的语境。

在过去的十年里，装置和影像艺术都已经变成一种世界语(lingua franca)，更准确地说，它是一种语法——它能够在世界范围内得以实践，每件作品讲述自己的本土语言或方言，也仍然能得到人们的理解。具有讽刺意义的是，中国权威把水墨画作为一种官方形式的艺术，这一焦点恰恰与西方关于纯粹价值观的讨论相对应：两者都提倡把一种中性的形式主义作为自由表达。关于中国文化的殖民主义和东方主义的观点在那里几乎已变成可以互换的概念。

在50年代期间，一种类似的关于自律性的讨论被美国搞成了美国抽象表现主义政治促销的基础。一本挑衅性的书，题为"纽约怎样偷窃现代艺术的观念"，毫无质疑地证实了抽象表现主义曾被联邦调查局利用，在二战后的欧洲为美国作宣传，根据的是关于纯粹价值的和先验性的讨论。一次又一次，帝国之争利用艺术去达到其各自的目的。一次又一次，艺术家们发明创造了独立性的策略去阻止，预防或反击此类事件。

在80年代早期，几乎是一夜之间，政治这个词不再容许进入艺术。我们再次被集中在绘画、雕塑上，在风格和所有的过时的价值上。那是个"疯狂绘画"的超前卫的时代。行为和影像艺术几乎从艺术舞台上消失。"政治"成为一个"非词汇"：成为更年轻一代的禁忌。这一代人显然厌倦了60、70年代流行的"做个好人之类"的词，他们想的是一夜暴富；想的是当金钱做主的时侯，不再被剥夺权利。"后现代主义"成为各取所需的新时期。

　　但是，1984年出现了一个有着深远影响的辩论的端倪，既所谓的"原始主义"的辩论，伴随着在纽约现代艺术博物馆的展览《二十世纪艺术中的原始主义，部落与现代性的姻亲关系》。由纽约现代艺术博物馆的 William Rubin 和 Kirk Varnedoe 策划，这是一次关于艺术史的展览。在那里非西方艺术和受到那些非西方艺术启发的西方艺术一起展出。有立体主义和超现实主义的绘画，作品来自贾科梅迪，恩斯特，塞尚等等。这些作品被认为是展览的明星；他们被展示在现代艺术馆的第一层楼，有着很好的光线和漂亮的空间。而所谓的原始性的作品——非洲的，大洋洲的，爱琴海的，美洲印第安人的以及很多非西方的其他作品（主要来自黑人的和太平洋文化）——被展示在入口。它们几乎没有被注解，被展示在光线昏暗的橱窗里。总之，它们除了作为西方艺术史或人类学的线索之外无关紧要。这次展览也包括了一个分开的部分，是年轻一代的西方艺术家的近期作品，有伊娃·海丝、罗伯特·史密森、以及理查德·朗。奇怪的是，他们和非西方的姻亲关系事实上无法得到证明。美国的批评家托马斯·麦克维利精彩地攻击了这次展览，他说："展示这些作品的唯一目的是证实'原始主义'是现代艺术中的一个思潮。同时，'原始性'反过来界定事实上的'部落物体'（tribal objects）"，他们没有尝试去揭示原始美学真实的内在意义。

　　据 McEvilley 看来，"原始性"呈现了批评家的确畏惧着某种东西。由此而把这些显然很优秀的艺术家们排除在 分离展之外，如约瑟夫·博伊斯或保罗·麦卡锡。由策划人Kirk Varnedoe撰写画册论文里宣布"回归自然的观念很危险地登陆"，并且这样的作品带出了"很不舒服的问题，即关于所有思想的终极内容是否计划从西方传统逃进一个原始性领域。"McEvilley 反击道："换句话说，原始性，是因为西方文明的利益而被删除出去的"。总之，这个展览暴露了我们的文化机构是怎样与外国文化产生联系的，也揭示了它作为一种种族中心主义的主观性已膨胀到如此地步，以至于把这样的文化（原始主义）及它们的物体纳入其（西方文化）自身内部。我所真正关心的是，这次展览表明了西方自我中心主义仍旧像在殖民主义和纪念品主义时代一样放纵。

　　像所有的检查制度一样，在西方艺术里，现代艺术馆关于"原始性"的检查制度是基于一种恐惧心理。我们不应低估这一恐惧，因为他像一条漫长的暗流贯穿西方文明。那种恐惧的本质是约瑟夫.科恩纳得的模棱两可的小说《黑暗之心》萦绕于怀的主题，小说被设定在20世纪初被比利时统治的刚果。在《黑暗之心》里，刚果的图景不是一个真实的非洲；它是一张恐惧地图，一个压抑的帝国忧郁的谵狂话语。一个深沉的裂痕潜藏于《黑暗之心》之中，似乎，背叛或自我厌恶的潜意识成了作者的爱国主义和收养他的英联邦的戏讽的镜像反射。它的主题被科波拉的电影《现代启示录》采纳不难理解，只是地点被改为越南。

　　自启蒙时代起，人的"阴暗面"、人具有天生邪恶的本质、自然社会是贪婪的、战争和暴力等主题一直困扰着西方文明。它被看成是自由需求的教条以及宗教和道德权威丧失的结果，其间伴随的是资本主义和自由民主运动的高涨。十八世纪的英国作家汤玛斯.霍布斯，在他的《利维坦》（Leviathan）中，首次发出了这样的声音，争论的反面当然是由卢梭的"贵族野蛮人"所呈现的，也就是说相信人本质上固有的优点。一项近期的研究表明卢梭熟知奴隶贸易，却决不会冒险要求废除奴隶制。

　　麦克维利在"原始主义"的辩论中最具启发也是最令人感兴趣的观点是，西方当代艺术自身显示出对"原始性"的恐惧和对激进与颠覆的恐慌之间存在着某种联系。也就是说对艺术所能引发和表现的我们社会中存在的深层问题之恐惧。恰恰不可预期的是，殖民主义与官方的、国家的或民族的艺术表征，通过删除"他者"的作用而被连接在一起。如果艺术在西方已被认为是一种"他者性"的显现的话，在最糟糕的情况下这也许会被解释为一个病态社会的症状（最显著的是在纳粹时期的"颓废艺术"）。那么在第三世界语境中出现的艺术构成某种"他者"的双重威胁。这个"他者"是非西方艺术家和知识分子必须与之抗争的、唯一的、并且是最富于挑战性的"神秘形像"。但是，如果要严肃地把它看作一种批判性艺术的话，它同样也是在西方艺术里，人们必须与之抗争的至关重要的神话。

相当一段时间以来，似乎这两种概念能够与后现代主义理论以及它正在成长中的伙伴——"文化研究"和"视觉文化"汇合，作为走出欧洲中心主义和新殖民主义的现代主义理论，它们偏好的就是"他者"的理论，都有能力包容西方和非西方的当代艺术。感谢像麦克维利样的批评家，后现代主义一度成为众多理论的汇流处，他们把法国哲学家福科、德里达、利奥塔、德勒兹·圭塔里，把解构主义理论，游牧主义理论和"根状茎"等等理论，融会贯通在西方和非西方的当代艺术中。但是，他也有弱点，因为后现代主义理论本身并不足够强大。它基本上依然是以欧洲为中心的，或是基于西方理论的，太折衷主义，太容易满足于各类"好"的和"不好"的艺术作品，过多地聚焦于带有异国情调的"多元文化"，无法对付所有非西方当代艺术的论题和他们特殊的历史性及图像体系。这些弱点在前面提到的《大地魔术师》的展览中显得格外严重。

这个展览由马尔丹（Jean Hubert Martin）策划，他当时任巴黎蓬皮杜中心现代艺术馆的馆长。这个展览的目的是对"原始主义"展览作一肯定的回答；通过使世界各地的当代艺术聚集一堂，站在平等的立足点上，从而驱除对"他者"的恐惧。策划人，艺术家，画廊经理，被送到世界最偏远的角落里去侦探当代艺术。这是一个巨大的，壮观的展览，很多作品从来没见过，这些艺术家也从没有听说过。它瞬间为艺术市场开辟了一个巨大的缺口。但它很不幸也是个很幼稚的展览。它的主要缺陷——不可宽恕的——是对非西方的作品没有提供上下文的关系，西方艺术的统治地位显而易见。并且这个展览是被它原打算与之抗争的诸种不合理现象所瓦解。批评潮涌而来，一年后马尔丹（Jean Hubert Martin ）的馆长职位被解除。然而，我们还是不得不感谢《大地魔术师》，很多非西方艺术家因此而成为国际艺术界的一部分，许多各式各样的展览也在试图做得更好。不过"魔术师们"还是必须承担指责，因为"非西方艺术"混杂在各类双年展和三年展中，官方的博物馆馆长或"独立策划人"继续飞来飞去，从墨西哥，中国，塞内加尔去挑选一两个"新"艺术家，他们将变成"下一次热门"。艺术家好像一直被留在这样的处境里，并且想尽办法使其作品能被看见和理解。

这些令我想起一断非常不同的历史，一段非常缓慢和隐蔽——在西方当代艺术中运作的与初期后现代主义和多元文化主义平行的历史。我指涉的是非西方人和移民以及本土的艺术家们漫长的艰苦奋斗的历史。这不是一种轻松愉快的工作也不是一种任性的折中主义，而是一种战斗，是一种必须对付各种形式的种族主义、外国人恐惧征、忽略和排斥的斗争。这种历史依赖于一小群相当有勇气的艺术家、批评家和收藏家的积极的前瞻性工作，像"第三重文本"，由 Rasheed Araeen 和 Jean Fisher 编辑的跨文化艺术杂志即以此命名，这是很多重要例证中的一个。

幸运的是，他们的影响已经得到越来越多来自其它研究领域的学术增援：历史和社会学，文化研究和文学理论。不可忽视的是我们目睹了揭示黑人奴隶史或黑色文化如何影响美国的调查研究。类似于萨义德所写的《东方主义》和《文化帝国主义》，或者由霍米·巴巴和斯皮瓦克发展的关于"他者"理论。艺术家们正在出版他们自己的批判性文本；我特别想提及的是由吉米·杜汉和郑明和的先锋性文本。今天，大量的文本可供我们阅读，我们很难以缺乏相应的材料为借口为自己的无知进行辩护。甚至更令人鼓舞的是，在艺术家和特别是年轻艺术家们和策划人之间，国际性的和知识上的交流越来越多，在艺术学院内，跨文化研究的兴趣日渐高涨。今天的批评家们来自世界各地，各种文化区域，来自巴基斯坦、印度、墨西哥、日本、南非等等，并且他们被要求策划重要的和主流性的展览。全球化和现代性的理论正在继续研究发展，也许有一天这一切会起到决定性的作用，不仅仅是在艺术上而且也可望在政治上有所影响。

这样一来，你会认为西方内部的情况已很明显地有所改善。但是对外国人的憎畏心理近来在欧洲有蔓延之势。并且普遍的情绪正在被两极化为"他们和我们之间"。回想一下民粹派和极右翼运动的上升趋势就足以说明问题。更糟的是沉默和无动于衷，那些有影响力的"官方的"艺术批评家和记者们认为不值得浪费他们的时间去调查研究那些"来自别处的艺术"，艺术仍然被置身于政治和意识形态的讨论之外。

非西方的艺术家们正在各处参与艺术的"公开声明"，从这一角度看，我们似乎有了些进步。但它是一个非常脆弱的过程，因为网络化和主观地加速健忘。大量的理论工作已经完成，这些几乎全部是由非西方的知识分子艺术家和批评家做的。它的大部分工作集中在创造一种有助于理解"他者艺术"的，介绍性的和为之抗争的系统。

但更多的要求是需要我们记录、研究、书籍和选集。我们需要分散艺术中心的权力；我们需要内行的西方艺术批评家和收藏家；我们更需要调查研究和记录现代性、现代主义和当代艺术在全世界的历史发展过程。在中国，很多艺术家和批评家之间的重要争论仍在继续，但中国的现代和当代艺术的历史仍然要从中国人自己的视野被书写。即使是日本，有着漫长的西化历史，它的现代生活方式和当代艺术和建筑，也从来没有制造出一本日本自己的现代艺术选集。今天谁能说谁是墨西哥社会主义壁画家的真正继承人？今天谁知道五十年代和六十年代早期在印度，埃及，土耳其和伊朗会有一个名副其实的现代性的萌芽？在历史被完全忘记或遗失之前，我们应该开始收集和书写更多的现代性历史。我的意思是，这样的历史性书写应该来自那些不同的"中心"和各个国家自己。为了理解我们今天看见的非西方艺术的发展趋势，真正的需要是逐步加强对其来源和语境关系，对其众多文字和图像的理解。

中国热在西方结束了吗？尽管参加《威尼斯双年展》和《文献展》的中国艺术家的数量日渐增多，再没有一个展览像《中国前卫艺术》或《另一个长征》那样在一段时间吸引了众多的注意力。但像《来自台湾的20位画家》或《来自格哈纳的三个女艺术家》之类的集体展时代已成过去，今天，展览已不再取决于"量"。更为重要的是像《合成现实》这类展览，由激情和策划人的精确度和第一手的历史知识构成的专业性的展览，由中国国内的和海外的艺术家共同营造。通过他们，中国当代艺术的历史将会逐渐成型。对于中国艺术家和批评家来说，前面的道路还很漫长。

合成现实

Els van der Plas

主题和形象界定了2002年12月《合成现实》展览的特征。在北京的这次展览中，大量的录像作品，数码媒体和音响充满了整个远洋现代艺术中心。这个巨大的、如同工厂一般的空间已经被改变成为充满活力的新媒体艺术展。参观者被大量录像影像和强烈的声音震撼，沉浸在这场展览中。这里不存在'观众的独裁政治'（2003威尼斯国际艺术双年展的主题），相反，观众们是被这些形象和空间的震撼力征服。

《合成现实》是中国首次大规模的关于影像和合成形象的展览之一。这些前卫艺术家，都是将近四十岁并且对中国艺术界及其他方面有着重要影响。他们是85运动（即新浪潮）的创始者和成员；是文化大革命后毕业的第一代艺术家，现在投身于自由创造和批判分析。他们也是1989年在中国美术馆举行的《中国前卫艺术展》的创导者。这次展览在开始的当天，因为两位艺术家在他们的作品上射击而被政府取消。89年后中国前卫艺术进入了历时数年的地下状态和非主流状态。其间表演，录像和概念艺术逐渐在中国社会找到了自己的道路。

艰难的文化发展在中国艺术领域留下了它们的痕迹。这种开放性和西方影响的混合、以及越发加剧的审查制度造就了这一代对现实存有矛盾态度的艺术家。什么是真实，一个特定的现实又是专门为谁设计的？今天，对于中国艺术家来说，最重要的问题之一涉及到他们用什么方式和日常现实（Everyday reality）关联。另外，在一个以缺乏自由见解为特征的国家中，现实的意义又是什么？《合成现实》既是这个问题的结论也是对将要面临的诸种新问题的预见。

陈绍雄（1962，广州）的录像向我们展示一座可弯曲的高楼正在躲闪一架加速飞行的飞机。这个图像使人立即意识到了9/11，并引起了人们对移动的大楼之惊奇。陈绍雄的作品关注当今国际恐怖主义，并在视觉上做了巧妙的处理。这一题为《视窗 2002》的作品不仅涉及那些观察美国这场大灾难的窗户而且影射比尔·盖茨的windows系统。我们看到的是真实的吗？这样的问题还能被提出来吗？在当今社会，虚拟现实正在扮演着越来越重要的角色。《合成现实》展览给耿建翌提供了一个探究展览现实界限的机会。展览的主题将新闻调查变成研究展览背后发生的事情。这些艺术家是谁？他们怎样生活？制造一个展览这一实践本身又意味着什么？在《有关"合成现实"》中，耿建翌展示了9个参展艺术家的"新闻式肖像"，分别在9台监视器上播放。《有关"合成现实"》关注的是制造（the making）和制造者（the makers）。从某种意义看，它有点像是一部Big Brother或"现实电视"节目（Reality TV）的艺术版本。朱加（1963，北京）实质上展示了一个与Big Brother原则相反的东西。2002年作品《双重风景》。用16mm彩色胶片记录一个年轻人坐在桌前喝咖啡的情景。我们可以通过他后面的窗户看到一些公寓街区。一个女士站在他前面，背对观众，那是服务生还是他的女朋友呢？尽管观众不易察觉，但事实上她是"伪造的"。那个喝咖啡的男人处在两个伪造的现实中：商店橱窗里的塑料"假人"和现代化城市，两者看起来都与历史无关，并且两者都仅仅传达着现代生活的"无聊"（the boredom of modernity）。实际上在电影里什么都没有发生：男人喝着他的咖啡,存在着的城市和一个虚假的女人。在这里"现实电视"(Reality TV)已经被消解为沉闷的影像。李永斌(1963,北京)创造了另一种'没有事件'的录像,被称作'阳光'。这一作品是由一个一小时循环的录像构成,拍摄的是一个冬天的窗户中太阳运动的轨迹。这个冗长的影像被配以一曲减速50%的巴赫音乐。李永斌似乎想拍摄"不可拍摄的现实"。他先前展出过一部可被称作"缓慢生存之美"的作品(《脸-3》)。在这一作品中,艺术家把他自己的脸投射在黑墨汁中,液体的运动把那西西斯(Narcissus)转换成一个怪物。《脸-1》是将一位老人的脸部肖像的幻灯片投映在自己的脸上再翻拍成录像。你在看什么?是一个老人还是年轻人,是男人还是女人?这些简洁的录像处理是李永斌作品的典型风格。王功新的《跨越》是另一种超现实主义,它是由录像和灯箱上的照片组成。照片反映的是艺术家骑车穿行于北京郊区。录像则展现了一个艺术家裸体飘在空中然后坠落于纽约街头。电影语言,尤其是科幻电影语言被使用于各种媒介,例如照片、移动影像、音响,以及对生活在"此处"与"别处"的空间场景处理。《跨越》戏剧化地表现了艺术家本人在世界最重要的两个城市—北京和纽约的自传式经历,并把问题引向移民与都市生活。

施勇创作"把形象作为现实"的艺术已经有一段时间了,他将夸大的现实和"陈词滥调"融入自己的创作中。在他的作品《上海形象》中,观众能用英特网挑选发型和中国男式服装。这里的问题是:"新式上海男人像什么?"。观众可以从中创造他们自己的现实。在《合成现实》中,施勇展示了他的视觉音响作品《QQ的幻觉》。一个打着各种手势的男人形象被投射在一张塑料薄膜上,裸露的扬声器放置在塑料薄膜的各个角落。这些手势产生猛烈的声音,屏幕因此震动起来。人物看起来似乎被放置在数码现实中。是幻觉还是错觉?QQ好像生活在Matrix世界:一个作为他自身想象力的囚犯,因制造炼狱而招来众魔。倪海峰(1964,舟山)展示了一个缩微现实。他展现了四个关于荷兰的缩微城Madurodam的录像。这一四通道装置由两个并置的投影与两个监视器构成。其中一个投影展示一个正像化了的倒影,伴随着现场环境声:各种杂音与一曲听似廉价的荷兰国歌(在Madurodam的一个机器里投入25欧分,你就可以听到荷兰国歌在一个微缩体育场里被无休止地播放)。其它三个通道录像分别记录这一"微缩现实"中的各种都市风景:机场、铁路、高速公路等。在这一题为《多重谎言》的录像装置中,真与伪似乎已不再是一个固定的二元对立。Madurodam城是在1952年由Willemstad,Curacao的Maduro夫妇为他们死于二战的儿子——Geogre建立的纪念碑。Geogre因他在战争早期的表现于死后被命名为荷兰国家英雄,Madurodam也由此成为他的人类学纪念碑。对倪海峰来说,这独特的历史和"这一缩微的国家"对于分析当今现实和历史的复杂性来讲是很有意思的材料。他把体现在Madurodam中的(荷兰的)民族主义看成某种"带有异国情调的东西"。这可与在一个西方人种学博物馆里对北京街道的表现相对比。这种"内向"的异国情调在海峰拍摄的画面中,例如那个缩微的司机刹车课程,显得如此荒诞。

汪建伟观察他自己的中国历史。他把关于共产主义时代的混杂记忆,包括现成品电影片段作为他的作品《布哈林是叛徒吗?》的原始材料。这里他选取了在中国倍受欢迎的赞美布尔什维克在俄国革命电影《列宁1918》中的片断。影片是由Mikhail Romm执导,其成功之作还有《十月列宁》的续集。在此汪建伟把历史与电影作为现实来处理,重新审视历史、电影、现实之间的关系；探讨电影是如何操纵或涂改我们的历史记忆的。这个多媒体影片包括影像图像，一个声道和一个灯箱照片，它被放置在一个像是电影院的黑暗空间。电影里的一个著名句子——看着我的眼睛，叠加在一个叛国者的肖像上。整个空间充斥着雷鸣般的革命修辞。历史事实的骄傲总被历史本身所代替。张培力的《遗言》也是取材于历史现成品，聚焦中国五六十年代电影中的英雄主义。张培力利用这些爱国影片中英雄们牺牲的场景，制作成分别是顺放和倒放的两个录像，两个录像被分别投射在两个相对的屏幕上。这样，站在空间中央，观众看到英雄在一边死去的同时又在另一边获得再生（毕竟，这些革命英雄是"不朽的"）。这些"电影中的现实"是中华人民共和国集体记忆的一部分。这些无止尽的牺牲和再生似乎是在揭示深藏于历史表现背后的意识形态话语的荒诞性。

《合成现实》展览反映出关注中国当代艺术已成为全球趋势的一部分。可说明这点的例子包括：1996 reckoning with the past，爱丁堡水果市场画廊的中国艺术展，1997《另一次长征，中国九十年代观念和装置艺术》，荷兰布拉达的中国概念艺术展，2001年威尼斯国际艺术双年展对中国当代艺术的广泛关注，还有2002侯翰如的Asian Vibe。另外，大量中国当代艺术展也开始在世界其它地区巡回。

《合成现实》将焦点集中在数码媒体和摄影录像艺术是一个革新，把一个如此之大的多媒体展览放在北京这一事实足以证明这是一个大胆的尝试。并且，艺术家们的初衷是确保这些原先大多呈现给海外观众的作品能回到中国本土。此次展览体现了艺术家们对数码媒体的热情及对"数码现实"的批判与分析精神。一个变化中的现实正在中国出现，《合成现实》的艺术家们分析、阐明与重构现实；《合成现实》代表着一种新的可能性。

关于"合成现实"的一段历史注释

皮力

今天,我们很难想象,录像艺术在1990年前后刚诞生的时候,它在中国到底意味着什么。录像艺术(VIDEO ART)尽管是一个外来的艺术门类。但是在中国的出现不简单是一个追随西方的结果。录像艺术在中国的产生是基于一定的文化状况才有可能发生的。确切的说,录像艺术在中国的出现,不单纯是艺术语言探索的结果,相反,录像艺术在中国的出现具有西方人难以理解的"意识形态性"和反"文化殖民"的色彩。

中国的录像艺术诞生于90年代前后,如果说过去官方的艺术让艺术家看到了艺术被政治所操纵的危险的话,那么为人们所熟悉的玩世现实主义和政治波普则使这些最早从事媒体艺术创作的艺术家感觉到架上绘画会受商业利益的驱使而被西方的新殖民主义利用的危险。而这两者都是基于旧式的艺术媒介和创作方法论。中国的录像艺术就是在这种背景下由当时相对年轻的艺术家提出并开始实践的。这些艺术家希望找到一种难以被西方画廊商业化的,但是又和主流艺术形成反差的艺术媒介。同时这种媒介又能允许个性化感觉和语言的存在,并易于使用、传播和交流。在这种情况下,录像艺术成为了他们的选择。

在年轻的艺术家看来,录像艺术在观看过程中所要求的时间性能导致比传统媒介中更深入的体验性。这种体验性能让作品获得超越文字描述的张力,即录像不能像现实主义的绘画那样被文字描述所穷尽,它要求观众的在一个时间段内的实际体验。同时录像装置的互动性能在欣赏的过程中邀请身体的进入。VIDEO ART在中文中被翻译为"录像艺术",这个名称还有更深的意义。录像的像蕴涵有REFLECT的意思。也许在当时的艺术家们看来,他们之所以使用录像作为一种媒体,在于录像艺术中蕴涵的REFLECT,它比传统绘画中那种简单的体验性,即RESPONSE 更加深入,也更符合艺术的本质。

正是在这种背景下,最早的几位录像艺术实验者首先面对的就是图像和心理与视觉体验之间的关系。他们希望通过对这些范畴的关注来改变因政治和意识形态的冲突而扭曲的中国当代艺术的面貌。朱加和张培力是同时也是最早的录像艺术实验者中的两位。在1991年,张培力就完成了他的第一件作品。他竭力强调录像艺术和大众电视节目的差别。所以他不允许任何常规手法、音效甚至电视的外形出现在自己的作品中。这种倾向在他著名的《不确定的快感》中看得更明显。而几乎与此同时,1994年,在北京的朱加则在尝试录像和新的生理体验之间的关系,他将摄像机绑在车轮上进行拍摄。这些无休止循环的图像被艺术家冠以"永远"的名字。这些作品是中国最早的录像作品,它们已经成为我们回顾这段历史时不可忽略的事实。无论是朱加还是张培力,他们都将行为作为自己作品一个基本点。和他们相似的是李永彬的作品,不同的是李的作品将"自己的"身体和身体体验作为不可替代的因素放在一个时间的维度中进行考察。这种"自我性"的修行使得我们对这些作品的观察充满了焦虑和不安。

同时,从另一个角度来说,中国录像艺术的发生同样也是建立在对90年代以前,国际录像艺术的反思上。也正是因此,中国的艺术家们往往将经典的录像艺术称作"标准的录像艺术”或者录像艺术的"枯燥传统"。更多的中国录像艺术家开始关注录像技术的可能性和这种可能性所给予的美学价值。在他们看来，标准的西方录像艺术作为一个经典，以及开始忽视新的、廉价的设备和技术为录像艺术带来的可能性。早期的西方录像艺术之所以在审美上有些枯燥，一方面是由于他们的反体制的思想，另一方面也是由于财力和技术原因。现在如果忽视技术发展和具体文化问题，将这种枯燥作为一种标准风格继承下来是愚蠢的，也是不能提供美学价值的。因此，中国录像艺术家开始发现对于标准录像艺术的追随将导致中国录像艺术失去自己存在的价值。在这种思想的指导下，录像艺术开始呈现出叙事性、互动性等几个新的方向。

作为对于标准的录像艺术的反思，叙事性被作为一种因素提出来。录像技术使录像分享了电影美学的许多成———种经典的电影时间处理手段适用于录像，不仅如此录像的时间处理在数字化方式下有着更大的弹性：各种数字特技制造的多种时间维度关系，大大丰富了传统电影语言，三维动画造型的介入更是使任何奇思异想却可能成为视觉现实。所有的这些赋于艺术家更多的可能性。对这种个人写作可能性一直保持清醒态度并展现出这种平民化写作方式的魅力的是汪建伟。在录像装置《链接》中他在一个走廊的两面分别播放由数部世界各国电影的盗版VCD中剪辑出来的暴力和色情电影片段构成的"新电影"和8个中国家庭观看电视的场面，他通过专业电影工作者最不以为然的简单方式，明了的揭示出我们的文化状况。汪挑战的不仅是标准的录像艺术也挑战了电影美学。重要的是他坚持数字技术的便捷和廉价性，而且他不失时机的利用廉价方式来制造新叙事并挑战商业和政治叙事中的廉价体验。

互动性实际上源于对于录像艺术的怀疑，即录像艺术是否最终还是会被电影美学和枯燥传统吞没？数码技术除了在像质、便捷方面的发展还能不能带来新美学价值。在这种追问下，录像装置作为一种"此时此地"的艺术受到艺术家的重视。因为录像装置在录像本身的属性之外更包含了装置所特有的品质，却又绝不止于是二者的总和。在空间中多重显示器播映多频录像或是多种投影形象在空间中按特定结构分布，在形象之间构成一种立体的戏剧性结构。中国录像艺术主要发展出两种性质的录像装置，分别偏重内在知识和内在体验。

偏重内在知识的录像装置往往是在具体的场景中，使录像形象与"道具"产生语义联系，既可以由图像来产生语义，也可以利用道具来进行点题。早年从事摄影和装置创作的倪海峰在《多重谎言》中，就是在图片和录像之间形成语义的转换，充分利用观众的知识判断来结构作品，同样在王功新的《婴语》中，投射在床上牛奶上的是不同的家人逗孩子时的表情，所有的牛奶从图像的口部流出再从其他地方循环回来。偏重内在体验的录像装置往往把观众身体运动的轨迹预先算计在装置结构内部的设计如陈绍雄早年的《视力矫正器》和施勇的《禁区》等。这类作品以人体工程学为依据，等待观众的身体从特定位置与路径上到来。身体被预设为一种影响到装置构成和现场情境本身的因素。围绕着来访者的身体通过而建立起来的现象世界不是作为外在知识，而是成为内在体验被唤醒。

录像装置都把互动性提上了议事日程，艺术家试图通过追求互动性来确定录像艺术的可能性。但是这有一些像"饮鸩止渴"，越是追求互动性，就越怀疑得录像艺术所能提供的空间。于是很多艺术家开始寻找录像装置以外的互动方式，偏重内在体验的艺术家开始放弃录像艺术，而希望借助新技术的可能性，于是更富技术色彩也更富设计色彩的互动多媒体艺术呼之欲出了。而偏重知识的则试图通过进一步打破媒介追求现场的或者心理层面上的互动。

通过录像艺术在中国的发展，我们可以看到，一个新的时代正在到来。西方的录像艺术产生是源于他们对体制的反叛，而在中国则是源于对媒介的关注。在西方1968年以后，随着基金会的介入，录像艺术的职业化在加强，在西方，过去20年人们不断的在切断它和电影、电视、摄影的联系，把它接纳进美术馆，这又导致了录像和装置的结合。经过这个时期，录像艺术由信息文化批判开始转向和社会思潮结合，从而使录像艺术获得自身的合法性。对于信息文化的批判是录像艺术的工作，但不是全部。个人化、手工化的当代艺术在本质上是不能和商业化信息媒介对话，更不可能驾驭它的。从1968年以前的录像艺术实践，我们可以看到，它和大众媒体的关系更像"一只强壮的苍蝇和苍蝇拍的关系"。中国录像艺术家和世界各国的录像艺术家一样，他们开始明白艺术家只能是在大众媒体鞭长莫及的地方找到自己的地盘和方式。

对互动性的追求是当代艺术的永远的梦想。但是我们也看到了，在对互动性的追求中，中国艺术家和世界的艺术家一样，他们中一部分在对录像这个媒体的开拓中，丧失了对于这个媒体的信心，最终走向了对媒体本身的背弃，走向了更富技术色彩也更富设计色彩的互动多媒体艺术。反对多媒体艺术存在和出现和对多媒体的盲目乐观同样可笑，但是中国录像艺术的现实使我们发现：如同录像艺术由信息文化批判开始转向和社会思潮结合，从而使录像艺术获得自身的合法性一样，现在是否又是需要重新连接它和电影、电视、摄影乃至更多的东西的时候。对于中国录像艺术而言，或许现在是选择的时候，我们究竟将录像作为一种媒介还是一种文化，因为不同的选择将导致进化论和多元论这两种截然不同的结果。

Chen Shaoxiong

1962 Born in Shantou, P.R.China
1984 Graduated from the print department of Guangzhou
      Fine Art Academy

Lives and works in Guangzhou,China

Solo Exhibitions
2003 Anti-C.S.X., Vitamin Creative Space, Guangzhou

Group Exhibitions
2003 *50th International Art Exhibition-Z.O.U. la*
      Biennale di Venezia
      Alors, La Chine? Centre Pompidou, Paris, France

      10th Biennial of the Moving Image Geneva,
      Switzerland
2002 *Pause-Gwangju Biennale* Gwangju, Korea
      New internationalism Kunstforeningen,
      Copenhagen, Danmark
      Urban Creation - Shanghai Biennale
      Shanghai Art Museum, Shanghai,China
      Under Construction Tokyo Opera City Art Gallery,
      Japan
      Synthetic Reality East Modern Art Centre ,Beijing
2001 *City Slang* He Xiangning Museum, Shenzhen
      Living in time-29 contemporary Artists from China
      Nationalgalerie im Hamburger Bahnhof, Berlin, Ger-
      many
2000 *Our Chinese Friends* Bauhaus-University and
      ACC Gallery, Weimar
      2nd Festival International d'Arts Multimedia Urbains
      Belfort, France
1999 *Cities on the Move 4,5,6,7*
      Louisiana Museum of Modern Art, Denmark;
      Hayward Gallery, London£¨ UK/
      The Finnish National Gallery, Helsinki, Finland
      Fast>>Forward New Chinese Video Art
      Contemporary Art Center, Macau
      9th International Photography Biennial Image
      Center, Mexico
      8th Biennial of Moving Images Saint-Gervais,
      Geneva
      Cities on the Move 2,3 CAPC, Bordeaux; Francee,
      PS1, New York,USA
1997 *Another Long March: Chinese Conceptual Art*
      Breda,The Netherlands

Geng Jianyi

1962 Born in Zhengzhou, P.R.China
1985 Graduated from the Oil Painting Department of
     zhejiang Academy of Fine Arts,

Lives and works in Hangzhou, China

Selected Solo and Group Exhibitions:
2003 *Alors, La Chine centre Pompidou*   Paris, France
2002 *GWANGJU Biennale* Gwangju, Korea
2001 *Living in time-29 contemporary Artists from China*
      Nationalgalerie im Hamburger Bahnhof,Berlin,Ger-
      many
2000 *Exit* Chinsenhale Gallery, London, UK
1998 *Inside Out : New Chinese Art, Exhibition of Art*
      from China, Taiwan and HongKong Asia Socity
      Galleries PS1, New York, /SFMoMA Asian Art
      Galleries, San Francisco, USA,
1998 *Two Contemporary Artists from China (together*
      with Zhou Tiehai) Presentation House Gallery,
      Vancouver, Canada
1997 *Cities on the Move* Secession, Vienna, Austria
      Another Long march-Chinese Conceptual and Instal-
      lation Art in the Nineties Chasse Kazerne, Breda,
      The Netherland
      China - Aktuelles aus 15 Ateliers Munich, Germany
1995 *Art Omi International Artists' Residency 1995*
      Omi Ghent, New York, USA
1993 *45th Biennale di Venezia-Passaggio ad oriente,*
      Nuova Pittura Cinese, Venice, Italy

Li Yongbin

1963 Born in Beijing, P.R.China

Lives and works in Beijing

Solo Exhibitions:
2000 *Li Yongbin Videos* Palais des Beaux-arts Brussels
Belgium
1996 *Video Art by Li Yongbin-August 30,1996* Cifa
Gallery, Beijing

Group Exhibitions:
2003 *Alors, La Chine?* Centre Pompidou, Paris, France
Artificial Respiration Zhen Miao Contemporary
Art Center, Beijing, China
2002 *Synthetic Reality* East Modern Art Centre, Beijing,
China
2001 *Clues to the Future* Red Gate Gallery, Beijing, China
Cross-Pressures Oulu Art Museum and Finnish
Museum of photography, Finland
This Is Me Ddmwarehouse Shanghai
Living in Time-29 Contemporary Artists from China
Nationalgalerie im Hamburger Bahnhof, Berlin,
Germany
2000 *Artists Writings* Gagarin volume second edition
1999 *Supermarket Art Show* Shanghai China
Autonomous Action In Artspace, Sydney
Signs of Life-Melbourne International Biennial
Melbourne, Australia
*Beyond the Future-Third Asia-Pacific Triennial of
Contemporary Art* Queensland art gallery,
Brisbane, Australia
1998 *Photography and Video From China* Max Protetch
Gallery, New York, USA
A New Form of Video Art in China 4A Gallery,
Sydney, Australia
Autonomous Action In Artspace, Auckland,new
Zeeland
1997 *Another Long March-Chinese Conceptual and Instal-
lation Art in the Nineties* Chasse Kazerne, Breda,
The Netherland
*Without Tile-Video Art Pilgrimage:Galerie Froment
& Putman* Paris, France
1995 *New Asian ART Show-1995* Kilin Plaza, Osaka,
The Japan Foundation Forum, Tokyo, Japan
1992 *New Wave. Chameleon Contemporary Art Space,
Hobart* Fire Station Gallery, Sydney, Australia

Ni Haifeng

1964 born in Zhoushan, P. R. China
1986 Graduated from Zhejiang Academy of Fine Arts (now
China Academy of Fine Arts)

lives and works in Amsterdam, the Netherlands.

Selected Solo Exhibitions:
2003 *Multiple lies* GEM, museum of contemporary art,
The Hague, The Netherlands
2002 *Airbag* Pond Paulus, Schiedam, The Netherlands
2001 *No-man's-land* Lumen Travo, Amsterdam, The
Netherlands
1997 *Anonymous* Gallery Gaby Kraushaar, Dusseldorf,
Germany
1996 *Secrets* Gate Foundation, Amsterdam,
The Netherlands
1995 *From Human to Humbug* Centrum Beeldende
Kunst, Leiden, The Netherlands

Selected Group Exhibitions:
2003 *In and Out* Dutch Contemporary Art 2003
National Museum of Contemporary Art, Seoul, Ko-
rea
2002 *Synthetic Reality* East Modern Art Center, Beijing,
China
ARTISSIMA (with Gallery Lumen Travo,
Amsterdam), Torino, Italy
Art Rotterdam Rotterdam Cruise Terminal,
Rotterdam, The Netherlands
2001 *Unpacking Europe* Museum Boijmans Van
Beuningen, Rotterdam, The Netherlands
1999 *Food for Thought* Mu Art Arctic Foundation,
Eindhoven, The Netherlands
1998 *Democracy* Gate Foundation, Amsterdam, The
Netherlands
1995 *Configura II* Gallery am Fischmarkt, Erfurt,
Germany
6. Triennale Kleinplastik Europa- Ostasien
Sudwest LB Forum, Stuttgart, Germany
1993 *Chinaese's New Art Post '89* Hong Kong Art Center,
Hong Kong
China Avantgarde Haus der Kulturen der Welt,
Berlin, Germany Kunsthal Rotterdam, The Nether-
lands / The Museum of Modern Art, Oxford, UK/
Kunsthallen Brandts Kleadefabrik, Odense, Denmark

Shi Yong

1963 Born in Shanghai, P.R.China

Lives and works in Shanghai

Selected Solo and Group Exhibitions:
2002 *Dream - the Contemporary Art Exhibition of China* Nanjing Museum, Nanjing,China
2002 Shanghai Biennale Shanghai Art Museum, shanghai, China
Money and Value, the Last Taboo Expo 02 Switzerland
XXV Biennale de Sao Paulo Sao Paulo Brazil
2001 *Unpacking Europe* Museum Boijmans Van Beuningen, Amsterdam, The Netherlands
Living in Time-Contemporary Artists from China Nationalgalerie im Hamburger Bahnhof, Berlin, Germany
Polypolis Art from Asian Pacific Megacities Kunsthaus, Hamburg, Germany
ARCO, ASIAN PARTY 1 , GLOBAL GAME Madrid, Spain
2000 *Leaving the Isaland-Pusan International Contempo-rary Art Festival* Korea
EXIT Chisenhale Gallery, London , UK
Looking out looking in Art Show 2 East Quad Art Gallery, University of Michigan, USA.
1999 *Food for thought* MU Art Foundation, Eindhoven, The Netherlands
Cities on the move 7 Kiasma, Museum of Contemporary Art, Helsinki, Finland
The Third Asia - Pacific Triennial of Contemporary Art Queensland Art Gallery, Brisbane. Australia
BM 99 BIENNALE DA MAIA Maia, Portugal
Cities on the move 4,5 Royal Festival Hall Hayward Gallery, London / Louisiana Museum of Modern Art, Denmark
1998 *JIANGNAN-Modern & Contemporary Art from China* International Exhibition Gallery, Vancouver, Canada
1997 *Cities on the move* Secession Art Museum, Vienna, Austria / Contemporary Art Museum of Bordeaux , France / P.S.1 Contemporary Art Center, New York, USA

Wang Gongxin

1960 Born in Beijing, P.R. China
1980 Bachelor of art, Capital Normal University, China

Lives and works in Beijing

Selected Solo and Group Exhibitions:
2003 *Echigo-Tsumari Art Triennial 2003* Japan
ARLES Photograph Festival 2003 Arles, France
Everyday - Contemporary Art from China, Japan, Korea and Thailand Kunstforeningen Copenhagen, Danmak
2002 *Metropolitan Iconographies - 25th Sao Paulo Biennial,* Sao Paulo, Brazil
Shanghai Biennial - 2002 Shanghai Art Museum, Shanghai, China
Tai Pei Biennial - 2002 Tai Pei Art Museum, Tai pei, Taiwan
Synthetic Reality East modern art center , Beijing, China
2001 *MAAP. 2001. Festival* IMA, Brisbane, Australia
Living in Time - 29 Contemporary Artists from China Nationalgalerie im Hamburger Bahnhof, Berlin, Germany
Translated Acts Haus Der Kulturen der Welt, Berlin, Germany/Queens Museum of art, New York, USA
Re:Duchamp, Travelling Exhibition / 2001 Venice Biennial, Venice, Italy
2000 *18th World Wide Video Festival* Amsterdam, The Netherlands
MAAP (Multimedia Art Asia Pacific) 2000 Festival. Power House Brisbane Australia
1999 *Revolutionary Capitals* The ICA. institue of con-temporary arts in London, UK
The Second Yearlong Contemporary Sculpture Exhibition He Xiang Ning Art Museum, Shenzhen, China.
1998 *Inside Out - New China's Arts* P.S.1 Institute of Con-temporary Arts, New York, U.S.A
1997 *Crack in The Continent* The Watari Museum of Con-temporary Art, Tokyo, Japan.
1996 *The Balance* Ifa Gallery, Bonn, Germany
Art as Gift The Bronx Museum of Arts, New York, USA
1995 *Contemporary Art from China* Santa Monica Art Center, Barcelona, Spain

Wang Jianwei

1958 Born in Sichuan, P.R. China

Lives and works in Beijing

Selected Solo Exhibitions:
2003 Walker Art Center,USA
1994 Accomplish Circulation-Sowing and Harvesting, Sichuan Province, China
1992 Hong Kong Art Center, Hong Kong
1991 Cultural Palace of Nationalities, Beijing, China

Selected Group Exhibitions:
2003 *CAMERA* Musee d'Art Moderne de la Ville de Paris, Paris, France
The 50th Venice Biennale Venice, Italy
Festival D'Automne Paris Pompidou Centre Paris, France
Multimedia Ceremony ICA London UK
2002 *The 25th Sao Paulo Bienial* National Pavilion, Sao Paulo, Brazil
Kunsten Festival des Arts Brussels, Belgium
2001 *Living in Time-29Contemporary Artists from China* Nationalgalerie im Hamburger Bahnhof, Berlin, Germany
Translated Acts Haus der Kulturen der Welt, Berlin, Germany / Queens Art Museum, New York , USA
2000 *Festival International de Programmes Audiovisuels* Biarritz , France
2000 Kunsten FESTIVAL des Arts Brussels Brussels, Belgium
Brighton FESTIVAL Brighton,UK
World Wide Video Festival Amsterdam, The Netherlands
1999 *Cities on the Move* Louisiana Museum of Modern Art, Humlebaek, Denmark / P.S.1 Contemporary Art Center, New York, USA / Hayward Gallery, UK London,
Melbourne International Biennial 1999 Melbourne, Australia.
Yamagata International Documentary Film Festival °Ø99 Yamagata, Japan.
1998 *Cities on the Move* Secession, Vienna, Austria/Musee d°Øart Contemporary de Bordeaus, France
1997 *Another Long March-Chinese Conceptual and Installation Art in the Nineties* Chasse Kazerne, Breda, The Netherland
The 10th Documenta Kassel, Germany

Zhang Peili

1957 Born in Hangzhou, P.R.China
1984 BA obtained from the Oil Painting Department, Zhejiang Academy of Fine Arts, Hangzhou

Lives and works in Hangzhou

Solo Exhibitions:
2000 Artist Project Rooms Arco 2000, Madrid,Spain
1999 Jack Tilton Gallery, New York USA
1998 The Museum of Modern Art, New York.,USA
1997 Galerie Krinzinger, Vienna, Austria
The Art Center, Centers of Academic Recources Chulalongkorn University, Bangkok, Thailand
1996 Video Forum Art 27 96, Basel, Switzerland
1993 Maison des Cultures du Monde, Galerie du Rond Point, Paris,France
Galerie Crousel-Robelin, Paris, France

Selected Group Exhibitions:
2003 *Z.O.U-Zone of Urgency -La Biennale di Venezia (50a Esposizione Internazionale d'Arte)* Venice, Italy
Happiness: A Survival Guide for Art and Life Mori Art Museum, Tokyo
10th Biennial of the Moving Image Geneve, Switzerland
Alors, La Chine Centre Pompidou Paris, France
2002 *PAUSE - Gwanju Biennale 2002* Gwangju, Korea.
MOIST-4th Multimedia Art Asia Pacific Festival Beijing, China
2001 *TELEVISIONS* Kunst Hall, Wien,Austria
Living in Time-29 Contemporary Artists from China Nationalgalerie im Hamburger Bahnhof, Berlin, Germany
2000 *Shanghai Biennale 2000* Shanghai Art Museum, Shanghai, China.
1999 *APERTO over ALL- La Biennale di Venezia (48a Esposizione Internazionale d'Arte)* Venice, Italy
Cities on the Move 4,5 Louisiana Museum of Modern Art, Denmark / Hayward Gallery, London, UK
1998 *Every day-11th Biennial of Sydney* Sydney, Australia
1997 *Another Long March-Chinese Conceptual and Installation Art in the Nineties* Chasse Kazerne, Breda, The Netherland

Zhu Jia

1963 Born in Beijing, P.R.China
1988 BA obtained from the Oil Painting Department, China
Central Academy of Fine Arts, Beijing

Lives and works in Beijing, China

Selected Exhibitions:
2003 *Beyond Boundaries* Shanghai gallery of Art (There
on the bund)
Alors, La Chine? Centre Pompidou Paris, France
*Z.O.U-Zone of Urgency -La Biennale di Venezia (50a
Esposizione Internazionale d'Arte)* Venice, Italy
Time After Time Yerba Buena Center for the Arts,
San Francisco, USA
2002 *Synthetic Reality* East Modern Art Center, Beijing,
China.
*Printemps de Septembre - Festival de Photographie
& Arts Visuels* Toulouse, France
Tempo The Museum of Moden Art , New York,USA
ASIANVIBE -An Exhibition of Contemporary Art
Espai d'Art Contemporani de Castello, Carrer Prim,
Spain
2001 *Living in Time-29 Contemporary Artists from China*
Nationalgalerie im Hamburger Bahnhof, Berlin,
Germany
*Translated Acts-Performance and Body Art from
East Asia 1990-2001* Haus der Kultren der Welt,
Berlin / Queens Museum of Art, New York,USA
2000 *Quotidian-The Continuity of the Everyday in 20th
Century Art* Castello di Rivoli-Museo d'Arte
Contemporanea,Torino, Italy
*PhotoEspana 2000- International Photography Fes-
tival of* Madrid, Madrid, Spain
1999 *The 3rd Art Life 21-SPIRAL TV - It's tomorrow now*
Wacoal Art Centre,Tokyo, Japan
Cities on the Move 4,5 Louisiana Museum of Monden
Art, Demmark / Hayward Gallery, London, UK
1998 *Every day-11th Biennale of Sydney* Sydney, Aus-
tralia
1997 *2nd Johannesburg Biennale* Johannesburg, South Af-
rica
*Another Long March-Chinese Conceptual and Instal-
lation Art in the Nineties* Chasse Kazerne, Breda,
The Netherland

陈劭雄

1962 生于中国广东省汕头市
1984 毕业于广州美术学院版画系

生活和工作在广州

个展
2003 "反—陈劭雄"，维他命创意空间，广州

主要群展
2003 *第50届威尼斯双年展主题展 紧急地带* 威尼斯，
      意大利
      第10届电影双年展 日内瓦，瑞士
      制造天堂 Le Parvis当代艺术中心，法国
2002 *"停"——光州双年展* 光州，韩国
      新国际主义 Kunstforeningen，哥本哈根，丹麦
      都市营造——上海双年展 上海美术馆，上海
      合成现实 远洋艺术中心，北京
2001 *城市俚语* 何香凝美术馆，深圳
      生活在此时 汉堡火车站美术馆，柏林，德国
2000 *我们的中国朋友* 鲍豪斯大学／ACC画廊，魏玛，
      德国
      第二届国际多媒体艺术节 Urbains Belfort，法国
1999 *移动中的城市（4、5、6、7）* 路易斯安娜当代艺
      术中心，丹麦／Hay ward画廊，伦敦，英国／曼谷，
      泰国／芬兰国家画廊，赫尔辛基
      第9届国际摄影双年展 墨西哥图像中心，墨西哥
      第8届电影双年展／日内瓦，瑞士
1998 *媒体转换:第11届柏林录像节* 波德维尔中心，德国
      移动中的城市（2、3）、CAPC，波尔多，法国／ P.
      S.1当代艺术中心，纽约长岛，美国
      16届世界录像节 阿姆斯特丹，荷兰
      另一次长征—中国观念艺术 布雷达，荷兰
      移动中的城市 Secession，维也纳，奥地利

耿建翌

1962 生于郑州市，中国河南省
1985 毕业于浙江美术学院油画系，

工作居住在杭州

个展
1999 *不可能取名* 上海香格纳画廊

主要展览：
2003 *啊! 中国* 巴黎蓬皮杜艺术中心
2002 *光州双年展* 光州，韩国
2001 *生活在此时-中国当代艺术家作品展* 汉堡
      火车站美术馆，柏林，德国
2000 *出口，中国馆* 英国伦敦
1998 *内部公开-来自中国，台湾和香港的艺术*
      纽约／旧金山，美国
      来自中国的两位艺术家（耿建翌和周铁海）
      展示厅画廊，温哥华，加拿大
1997 *移动的城市* 分离派艺术馆，维也纳，奥地利
      永恒与时尚 -在变化的环境中的中国当代艺术
      东京，大阪，日本
      另一次长征-90年代中国观念艺术 荷兰基础
      基金会
1996 *中国-15位艺术家联展* 德国慕尼黑
      中国前卫艺术家 巴塞罗那圣莫尼卡艺术中心
1995 *艺术* 欧迈艺术中心，国际艺术家村，纽约
1993 *中国新绘画-第45届威尼斯双年展* 威尼斯，意
      大利

李永斌

1963 年出生于北京

现生活工作在北京

集体展览：
2003 *啊！中国* 蓬皮杜艺术中心,巴黎,法国
2002 *我的空间* 山西,平遥国际摄影艺术节
     合成现实 远洋现代艺术中心,北京
2001 *矛盾中的北京* 芬兰, 奥录美术馆, 赫尔辛基摄
     影美术馆
     迹象未来 北京,红门画廊
     生活在此时 汉堡火车站美术馆,柏林
     这是我 上海,东大明创库画廊。
2000 *李永斌的录像作品* Palais des Beaux—arts布鲁
     塞尔,比利时
1999 *超市* 上海,中国
     独自行动 澳大利亚,悉尼,Artspace
     生活的痕迹－墨尔本双年展 澳大利亚,墨尔本
     超越未来"亚太地区三年展 昆士兰美术馆,澳大
     利亚
1998 *中国摄影和录像艺术* Max Protetch画廊,纽约
     来自中国的录像艺术 4A画廊,悉尼,澳大利亚
     独自行动 Artspace,奥克兰,新西兰
1997 *另一次长征－中国观念艺术展* 布瑞达,荷兰
1996 *影像巡礼* Froment & Putman画廊,巴黎
1996 *李永斌的录像作品* 中央美术学院画廊,北京
1995 *新亚洲艺术展／大阪,东京,日本*
1994 *94'北京,中、日、韩当代展艺术展* 首都师范大
     学, 北京

倪海峰

1964 年生于中国浙江省舟山市
1986 年毕业于浙江美术学院（现中国美术学院）

生活和工作在荷兰阿姆斯特丹。

个人展览：
2003 *多重谎言* GEM当代艺术博物馆, 荷兰海牙
2002 *空气袋－倪海峰个展* Pond Paulus, 荷兰斯黑丹
2001 *无人之城* Lumen Travo画廊,荷兰阿姆斯特丹
1997 *匿名* Gaby Kraushaar画廊,德国杜塞尔多夫
1996 *秘密* Gate基金会,荷兰阿姆斯特丹
1995 *From Human to Humbug* 莱顿视觉艺术中心,荷兰

集体展览：
2003 *In and Out 荷兰当代艺术2003* 国立当代美术
     馆,韩国汉城
2002 *合成现实* 北京远洋艺术中心,中国北京
     海市蜃楼 苏州美术馆,中国苏州
     ARTISSIMA艺术博览会 意大利都灵
     鹿特丹艺术博览会 Rotterdam Cruise Terminal,荷
     兰鹿特丹
2001 *打开欧洲* Boijmans van Beuningen 博物馆,荷兰鹿
     特丹
1999 *精神食粮* Mu 艺术基金会,荷兰埃恩霍恩
1998 *民主* Gate 基金会,荷兰阿姆斯特丹
1995 *第二次构型展* Fischmarkt画廊,德国伊尔福特
     东方与西方 西南LB论坛,德国斯图加特
     现代艺术博物馆,路德维戈基金会,奥地利
     平衡 德国对外文化交流协会,德国斯图加特
1993 *后89中国新艺术* 香港艺术中心,香港
     中国前卫艺术展 柏林世界文化宫,德国柏林／
     鹿特丹艺术馆／荷兰鹿特丹,牛津现代美术馆,英
     国牛津

施　勇

1963　出生于上海

现生活和工作在上海

主要展览
2002　白日梦－中国当代艺术展　南京博物院,南京
　　　上海双年展　上海美术馆,上海
　　　金钱和价值－最后的禁忌　瑞士艺术博览会
　　　第二十五届圣保罗双年展　圣保罗,巴西
2001　被打开的欧洲　Boijmans Van Beuningen 美术馆,
　　　荷兰
　　　生活在此时　柏林,德国
　　　城市与城市　艺术之屋,汉堡,德国
　　　亚洲的舞会 世界的游戏　马德里当代艺术博览
　　　会,马德里,西班牙
2000　离开孤岛　釜山国际当代艺术节,釜山,韩国
　　　出口　CHISENHALE画廊,伦敦
　　　看外面,看里面　上海当代艺术展2
　　　EAST QUAD画廊,密歇根大学,美国
1999　精神食品　荷兰MU艺术基金会,爱恩霍因,荷兰
　　　移动中的城市6　KIASMA 当代美术馆,赫尔辛基
　　　第三届亚太当代艺术三年展　昆士兰美术馆,布
　　　利斯班
　　　99玛雅当代艺术双年展　玛雅,葡萄牙
　　　移动中的城市4,5　HAYWARD 画廊,伦敦
　　　LOUISIANA 现代美术馆,丹麦
1998　江南－现代与当代中国艺术展　GRUNT 画廊,温
　　　哥华
1997　移动中的城市1,2,3　P.S.1当代艺术中心,纽约/
　　　波尔多当代艺术博物馆,波尔多／"分离派"美
　　　术馆,维也纳
1996　让我们谈谈钱－首届上海国际传真交流展　上海
　　　华山美校画廊
　　　以艺术的名义－中国当代艺术交流展　刘海粟美
　　　术馆,上海
1995　非此处,非彼处－　施勇,钱喂康艺术访问展
　　　ACCESS艺术家竞争中心,温哥华
　　　同意以45。作为理由　杭州,上海,北京非定点
　　　艺术活动,艺术家居室空间

王功新

1960年　出生于北京
毕业于首都师范大学

现生活和工作在北京

个展
2002　《王功新来自北京》个展　南澳当代艺术中心　澳
　　　大利亚
　　　《"BIAO"》个展　Halle10艺术中心 路德维西堡
　　　德国
　　　《打井》个展　No.12报房工作室 北京

主要展览
2003　亚洲媒体艺术的未来　广岛市立当代美术馆 日本
　　　越后妻有艺术三年展　日本
　　　2003年阿尔乐国际摄影节　阿尔乐 法国
　　　每一天－国际艺术中心　哥本哈根 丹麦
2002　五届圣保罗双年展 圣保罗 巴西
　　　2002年上海双年展 上海美术馆 中国
　　　2002年台北双年展 台北美术馆 台北
2001　2001年亚太多媒体艺术节　当代艺术中心 布里斯
　　　班 澳大利亚
　　　生活在此时,汉堡火车站国家美术馆 柏林,德国
　　　行为的转移 文化宫美术馆,柏林,德国／皇后
　　　美术馆,纽约,美国
　　　旅行中的杜尚－2001年威尼斯双年展　威尼斯,
　　　意大利
2000　第18届世界录像艺术节 阿姆斯特丹,荷兰
　　　2000年亚太多媒体艺术节 布里斯班 澳大利亚
1999　革命的都市 ICA 当代艺术中心,伦敦,英国
　　　第二届国际雕塑展 何香凝美术馆,深圳
　　　由内至外－新中国艺术展　P.S.1当代美术馆
　　　纽约 旧金山当代美术馆,旧金山,美国
1997　大陆的裂痕　和多利当代美术馆 东京,日本
1996　平衡　IFA美术馆,司徒加特,波恩,德国
　　　礼物艺术　布朗士美术馆,纽约,美国
1995　中国当代艺术展　Santa Monica 当代艺术中
　　　心,巴塞罗那,西班牙

汪建伟

1958 年 10 月生于中国四川

生活和工作在北京

个人展览
1991　*汪建伟个人展*　北京民族文化宫，中国
1992　*汪建伟个人展*　香港艺术中心，香港
1994　*种植—循环*　四川，中国
2003　*汪建伟个人展*　美国沃克艺术中心，美国

群展
2003　*影 室*　法国巴黎市立现代艺术美术馆
　　　第50届威尼斯双年展　意大利威尼斯
　　　巴黎秋季戏剧节　法国巴黎蓬皮杜艺术中心
　　　多媒体戏剧"仪式"在英国ICA上演
2002　*第25届圣保罗双年展*　巴西，圣保罗
　　　2002布鲁塞尔戏剧节　比利时布鲁塞尔
2001　*状态*　德国柏林艺术展览中心
　　　行为的传译　德国柏林世界艺术宫/
　　　美国纽约皇后博物馆
　　　生活在此时　德国柏林汉堡火车站美术馆
2000　*法国国际影像节*　法国巴瑞思
　　　2000布鲁塞尔艺术节　比利时布鲁塞尔
　　　布莱顿艺术节　英国布莱顿
　　　世界影像节　荷兰阿姆斯特丹
　　　上海国际双年展　上海美术馆
1999　*移动的城市*　丹麦哥本哈根Louisiana当代博物馆/
　　　美国P.S.1当代艺术中心/
　　　英国伦敦Hayward画廊
　　　墨尔本国际双年展　澳大利亚墨尔本
　　　第十届日本山形国际电影记录片节　日本山形
1998　*移动的城市*　法国波尔多现代艺术馆
1997　*又一次长征—中国当代艺术1997*　荷兰布瑞德
　　　第十届文献展　德国卡塞尔
1996　*第二届亚太地区当代艺术三年展*　澳大利亚昆士
　　　兰美术馆
1995　*新亚洲艺术展—1995*　日本大阪，日本东京
　　　95光州双年展　韩国光州
1994　*中、韩、日'94北京国际交感艺术展*　北京首都
　　　师范大学美术馆

张培力

1957 年 11 月生于杭州
1980–1984年就读于中国美术学院(原浙江美术学院)

生活和工作在北京

个人展览
2000　马德里当代艺术博览会（Arco）"艺术家空间"，
　　　西班牙
1999　纽约 杰克.丢顿(Jack Tilton) 画廊，美国
1998　纽约现代艺术博物馆，美国
1997　维也那 Krinzinger 画廊，奥地利
　　　曼谷 Chulalongkom 大学美术馆，泰国
1996　巴塞尔第27届当代艺术博览会"录像论坛"，瑞士
1993　巴黎 世界文化宫　Rond Point 画廊，法国
　　　巴黎 Crousel–Robelen 画廊，法国

主要群展
2003　*第50 届威尼斯双年展——紧急地带*　威尼斯，
　　　意大利
　　　快乐：艺术及生活的生存指南　东京莫里美术
　　　馆，东京，日本
　　　第十届影像双年展　日内瓦，瑞士
　　　啊！中国　巴黎蓬皮杜艺术中心，巴黎，法国
2002　*暂停*　韩国光州双年展　光州，韩国
　　　润化－亚太媒体艺术节　北京中华世纪坛艺术
　　　馆，北京，中国
2001　*电视－视觉*　奥地里维也纳艺术宫
　　　生活在此时　柏林国立汉堡火车站当代美术馆，
　　　柏林，德国
2000　*上海双年展 2000*　上海美术馆，上海，中国
　　　穿墙人－中国当代艺术新景象　法国亚眠，庇
　　　卡底国家美术馆
1999　*全面开放－第48 届威尼斯双年展*　意大利威尼斯
　　　Giardini公园，意大利馆，威尼斯，意大利
　　　回顾与展望－2000莱因河畔的全球艺术　德国
　　　波恩艺术博物馆，波恩，德国
　　　起源点 –1950–1980 年代全球观念艺术　美国
　　　纽约 Queens艺术博物馆
　　　表皮－深度－当代艺术中的外观与外表　耶路
　　　撒冷，以色列博物馆，以色列
　　　移动的城市4,5　路易斯安娜现代艺术博物馆，
　　　丹麦/伦敦 Hayward 画廊，英国
1998　*每天－澳大利亚悉尼第十一届悉尼双年展*
　　　移动的城市2　当代艺术博物馆，波尔多，法国

朱加

1963 年生于北京
1988年毕业于中央美术学院 油画系

生活和工作在北京

主要展览
2003 一次又一次亚洲和我们的时刻　　旧金山当代
艺术中心，美国
理想与冲突－紧急地带　第50届威尼斯双年展
阿森纳利，威尼斯，意大利
啊！中国　巴黎蓬皮杜艺术中心
界线之外　上海外滩3号画廊
2002 *震动：一个来自亚洲的当代艺术展*　Espai d'Art
Contemporani de Castello,西班牙
节奏　纽约现代艺术博物馆，纽约，美国
九月的春天　图鲁兹，法国
合成现实　远洋现代艺术中心，北京
2001 *行为的转译*　柏林世界文化宫／纽约皇后美术馆
生活在此时－来自中国29位当代艺术家的作品展
汉堡火车站当代艺术博物馆，柏林
2000 *抽取－在20世纪的艺术中延续一个概念*
Castell di Rivoli－Museo d Arte contemporanea,都
灵，意大利
影像西班牙2000－中心的边缘　马德里，西班牙
1999 *The 3rd Art life 21－Spiral Station－SPIRAL TV*　东京
华歌尔艺术中心，日本
拓开的真实－中国当代摄影　精艺轩画廊，温哥
华，加拿大
Un matin du monde
Eric Dupont 画廊，巴黎，法国
移动的城市4,5　　路易斯安纳现代艺术博物馆，
丹麦，海沃德画廊（Hayward Gallery），伦敦，
英国
1998 *16届World Wide 录像节*　阿姆斯特丹,荷兰
每一天－第11届悉尼双年展　悉尼,澳洲
移动的城市2,3　波尔多当代艺术博物馆,法国／
P.S.1当代艺术中心，纽约，美国
1997 *第2届约翰内斯堡双年展*　约翰内斯堡,南非
移动的城市／维也纳 SECESSION，奥地利
另一次长征－中国九十年代观念和装置艺术　布
雷达Chasse Kazerne，荷兰

Colophon

This publication and exhibition by the same title, have been made possible by the generous support of the Prince Claus Fund for Culture and Development, The Netherlands and Mr. Guo Hongyong.

Special thanks to: the participating artists, Marianne Brouwer, Els van der Plas, Thomas J. Berghuis, Pi Li, John Blake, Huang Zhuan, East Modern Art Center.

Publisher: Timezone 8 Limited
28/F No.3 Lockhart Road Hong Kong
e: info@timezone8.com
http://www.timezone8.com

Editor: Ni Haifeng, Zhu Jia
Texts: Marianne Brouwer, Els van der Plas, Pi Li
Translation: Wu Zi, Cindy Carter
Text Correction: John Blake
Photography: the artists, Zhu Jia, Ni Haifeng
Design: Ni Haifeng, Zhu Jia
Project initiator: Zhu Jia, Ni Haifeng
Printing: Beijing Youth Cultural Transmission Ltd.
Size: 170mm x 240mm

ISBN: 988-97262-0-3